Road to Belonging is a beautiful and poignant memoir of Lynne's life as an adopted person that illuminates the complexities and lifelong impact of the 'Closed Adoption' practice in Aotearoa NZ. She normalises the desire to know one's roots and what that journey can be like for all parties in the adoption circle once embarked upon.

Lynne doesn't shy away from the 'darkness' of the adoptive experience and offers hope that with faith, support and when our human need for love and kindness is met, it can change so much. Lynne also shines a light on a thread of enduring love and faith in God that can weave its way through our day-to-day lives and sustain us through whatever we endure if we look for it.

This special book offers both adopted and non-adopted people valuable and deeper insight into the adoption experience, the power of faith, and the sensitive nature of reunion.

—**Jo Willis**
Personal Development and Leadership Coach
www.jowilliscoach.com

Growing up with my mother secretary for 26 years of Childhaven, a home for unmarried mothers, I was familiar with the girls' side of the story. They did not give up their babies easily but were forced by the social attitudes of the times—and sheer financial necessity.

To read Lynne's poignant account of being an adopted child opened my eyes to what it meant to her to be part of a loving family yet needing to know the truth about her birth mother so that she could discover her full identity.

This is a book that should be read by everyone concerned with adoption.

—**Elaine Blick**
Author of *First Names Only*

Road to Belonging is a heartwarming account of the delicate topic of the issues surrounding closed adoption. Lynne invites us into her intimate experiences of reconnecting with her birth parents and what it means to weave a family out of biological and non-biological kin. It is both challenging and inspiring, giving us glimpses into Lynne's deeply held faith as an anchor for her soul. As a counsellor, I can sense her soul's yearning to know who and whose she is, since attachment is at the heart of being human. From a place of shame and secrecy to a spacious place of belonging, this book is sure to inspire anyone who knows someone or has had a similar experience.

—**Ruth Lawson-McConnell PhD**
www.ruthmcconnell.com

This is a beautiful story of love, family, and belonging, eloquently narrated by Lynne as she shares the struggles and joys of searching for her birth parents. There is a Māori whakataukī *Kia whakatōmuri te haere whakamua* which means 'I walk backwards into the future with my eyes fixed on my past'. It tells of how our ancestral history remains with us always as part of our present life. I admire Lynne's generosity in sharing her journey towards reconciliation with her lost family and commend her on taking that "handful of courage and hope" to walk backwards into her future.

—**Dr Nikki Kiyimba**
Clinical Academic and Trauma Specialist

A poignant, tender story that touches your heart. Told with simple honesty and no trace of bitterness, the painful questions, the deep yearning for family connection, and ultimately the life-changing answers weave a beautiful hope-filled story of healing and restoration.

—**Rosie Boom**
www.rosieboom.com

Identity and belonging—the need to know who we are, and that we are loved, are basic components of our wellbeing. Lynne's poignant description of her brave journey to reclaim these attributes is an inspiration. Her story sheds light on the human condition and will provide comfort and hope for many.

—**Alistair Reese PhD**
Farmer, Historian and Theologian

A vulnerable true-life story of a gentle and gracious woman who found the courage to search for hidden pieces of her life's puzzle. Lynne made a choice to search for truth, even when it was hard, hoping it would bring healing to the unexplained pain deep in her heart. Her story helps others to realise their feelings and story matter too. Everybody's does.

Lynne and her husband Phil have been inspirational to us; the love, devotion, fun and commitment in their family is second to none. They have created a place of belonging—where everyone is valued, loved and accepted . . . just what Lynne's heart always longed for.

—**Donna and Jonny Boom**
Lead Pastors, Changepoint Church, Tauranga, NZ

Road to Belonging

TORN CURTAIN PUBLISHING
Auckland, New Zealand
www.torncurtainpublishing.com

ISBN Softcover 978-1-991299-19-2
ISBN ePub 978-1-991299-20-8

All scripture quotations in this publication are taken from the New King James Version. Copyright © 1982 by Thomas Nelson, Inc. Used by permission. All rights reserved.

Some names and identifying details of people described in this book have been altered to protect their privacy.

Typeset in Playlist, Raleway, Minion Pro, Berlin Sans

Cataloging in Publishing Data
 Title: Road to Belonging
 Author: Lynne Leppard
 Subjects. Pregnancy and Adoption; Closed Adoption; Identity; Faith; Family Life; Family History; Pastoral Issues; New Zealand history; Healing and Restoration.

A copy of this title is held at the National Library of New Zealand.

Road to Belonging

Establishing a Legacy of Love after Closed Adoption

Lynne Leppard

Dedicated to my grandchildren
May you feel loved, nurtured and cared for,
like every child deserves.

Foreword

IN *ROAD TO BELONGING*, Lynne Leppard courageously shares her journey of being born in a time when closed adoptions were kept a secret—full of shame, rejection and abandonment. She openly shares her struggle and determination to find answers, inspiring us with her courage as she seeks out relationships with her mother and father and their whanau, despite the pain involved. Along the way, God gives her a soulmate in Phil, creating a secure place for Lynne to acknowledge and attend to festering wounds. Her subsequent healing is evidenced by her own warm mothering of five children and her expanding whanau. God's grace and provision towards Lynne in her journey are clearly revealed as she seeks his face and learns of his love for her.

In my professional life, I have had the privilege of working alongside many families, including babies given up by mothers who stayed in NICU, and their adoptive parents. My Master's thesis focused on adoptive parents bonding with children from Russian orphanages, so I truly resonated with Lynne's story. It brought tears to my eyes as I read of her pain, but also smiles as I witnessed God's grace and love woven throughout her journey.

Attachment theory states that a child develops optimally in a parent-child relationship via an ongoing cycle of needs being met and trust being established. When a baby expresses their need and is soothed, the world as they know it becomes a safe place. They develop trust and a sense that all is well in their world. When this cycle is disrupted, a child fails to internalise the sense of safety that a consistent caregiving relationship is meant to establish.

Like Lynne, every adopted child experiences disrupted attachment. A baby taken away from the mother who gave them life imbues a sense of insecurity and loss, leading to an experience of abandonment and rejection. The former practice of closed adoptions severed any ongoing relationships between natural parents and adoptive parents, and also excluded professionals from facilitating any discussion, acknowledgement, grief processing, and proactive attachment relationship practices for adoptive parents.

In contrast, Jesus reaches out to vulnerable people who feel unattached and unloved—as seen in his gift of healing for the woman at the well. In caring for her needs, he demonstrated his role as the *ultimate attachment figure* for all 'unattached' people. Jesus himself understands rejection and shame, thus identifying with adopted people who experience first the loss of their mother who carried them in utero, and then the ongoing loss and shame of a closed adoption or an orphanage.

Lynne's life is a testament to God reaching through trauma with a hand of hope to weave a legacy of love. Like David in the Psalms, Lynne chose to be real with God, openly exploring her own infancy and childhood so she could understand the attachment paradigm through which she thought and behaved. This honest examination of her past enabled her to make changes for both present and future relationships.

Lynne's story will resonate for anyone who has experienced insecure attachments, losses and trauma, and inspire readers to explore their own past, while seeking a secure base in the present. It also invites us to allow God to speak to each of us of his unconditional love as a Father. His care for us is evident in Jesus who paid the ultimate price to bring us freedom, and the Spirit who holds, walks alongside and carries each one of us as a parent should.

God gives children parents in order to model his love for them. Yes, as parents we too often fail to provide fully for our children's emotional needs, but God reaches out with love and grace to restore all that we bring before him and to enable us, like Lynne, to create our own 'legacy of love'.

Road to Belonging provides a wonderful understanding of the realities of closed adoption and the possibilities for trust and security to be re-established. I warmly recommend Lynne's book to all.

—Jocelyn Johnstone
RN, Plunket Nurse, Dip Couns, MA (Community & Family)

Contents

Introduction

I WAS SPENDING A few days with a group of my closest friends by the pristine waters of Lake Taupo. It was a weekend of girl talk and eating out, a time set aside for relaxing and catching up with each other, and since it only came around once a year, we had all been looking forward to it.

After an enjoyable dinner we returned to our holiday accommodation near the water's edge, where we continued our conversation, reminiscing about how our lives had been woven together over the years. The conversation soon evolved into a discussion about how many of the circumstances that had brought us together seemed unexplainable, and, as is often the case, the topic of families came up. Having been adopted as a baby, I was aware my family dynamics were a little more unusual than most, and although I had been searching for answers for many years I still had limited information about my history and lineage.

This is because I was born during the years when 'closed adoption' was a policy in New Zealand. Under the *Adoption Act* of 1955, people who were adopted from that year onwards were prohibited from accessing any official information regarding their biological parents and family. In fact, it wasn't until the passing of the *Adult Adoption Information Act* in 1985 that adoptees (aged 20 or above) were granted the right to formally seek identifying information about their biological parents.

As we talked, I shared with my friends how I felt like a detective trying to piece together all the parts of the puzzle. Although the change in law now allowed adult adoptees to seek information about their heritage, there seemed to be an obstacle at every turn. I had always been curious about my heritage, but the secrecy and shame that surrounded adoption at the time of my birth made the search for my biological family incredibly frustrating.

My friends were initially silent as they contemplated everything I had shared, but as they thought about it, they began expressing how normal it was for them to know the details of their background, or at least to easily find information about their heritage if they wanted to. I, on the other hand, had never met my birth family and had no records telling me who I was or where I came from. Under the Adoption Act, those files were sealed away, and the only hope of gaining access to them was by applying to the courts. Years later, the courts reluctantly released those documents to me, but by then they told me little I didn't already know. For now, I was still searching, hoping that one day I would find the information about my heritage that I was desperately looking for—information that my friends simply took for granted. What I did not know was that it would take many more years (and many ups and downs along the way) before the puzzle pieces of my identity would slowly start to come together.

IN 1965, WHEN I was born, adoption was the usual pathway for an unmarried woman with a surprise pregnancy. There were two reasons for this. It was deemed improper for babies to be born into circumstances where their parents weren't married, and there was no support available unless family stepped in—which was uncommon, even though they were kin. And so, when I was just seven weeks old, I was adopted. With all records kept confidential, nobody had access to information about where I was going or where I had come from. All my family ties were essentially cut.

You may be wondering about the effects of closed adoptions on those involved. There are many adoption stories out there, and people tend to be curious about the ripple effects on the adoptee, their birth parents, and their adoptive parents and families. These stories are often spun in an ultra-positive 'happy ever after' narrative, or conversely, painted in a negative light detailing lives ruined by misfortune. I have since learned that most real-life experiences of adoption fall somewhere in between.

When I was younger, I struggled with my sense of identity and belonging as I pondered being part of two different families—biological and adoptive. This was my 'normal', yet few could understand how I felt. For many years, I felt wounded—only it seemed there was no way to bind the wound or apply the healing balm I so desperately longed for. I would have appreciated someone with their own adoption experience coming alongside me during that time to offer their support and wisdom as I contemplated these things. It is my hope in sharing some of my own, very personal experiences of life as an adoptee, that I might bring further awareness and understanding about the process of closed adoption to others and offer hope to anyone involved in the adoption triad that healing and wholeness is ultimately possible.

1

What's in a Name?

MY STORY BEGINS IN the summer of 1965, just before Christmas, when a young woman left Childhaven, a New Zealand home for unmarried mothers, and travelled to Saint Helen's Hospital to give birth. A few hours later, I was born. Yet any joy my mother may have felt at my arrival would have likely ebbed away as reality sank in. A single woman with little or no support, she had already made the heart-wrenching decision to place me for adoption. Within days, a foster family was found, and my mother left the hospital without a baby in her arms.

I spent the earliest days of my life in foster care. Once a week, my mother caught a bus to my temporary home, fitting in as many visits as she could before I disappeared from her life—presumably, forever.

❧♡☙

THE MATRON OF CHILDHAVEN and the secretary, Evaline, were still looking for a home for me when, at six weeks of age, I was admitted to a hospital for 'persistent crying' and with what the doctors termed 'failure to thrive'. For some reason, which is still unclear to me, my appendix was removed while I was there. It was the first of many unknowns that I would wonder about in the years that followed.

Just before I was discharged from the hospital, Evaline's husband was invited to speak at a church in another part of the country. Having travelled a fair distance, they arranged to stay for the weekend with their close friends Ralph and Muriel. After the service that Sunday, while the two couples were enjoying lunch, Evaline explained to Ralph and Muriel that a young single mother at Childhaven was looking for a Christian family to give her baby a home. "Would *you* consider adopting another little girl?" she asked them.

Ralph and Muriel were surprised. They had met at a church camp in their twenties and married after their courtship, and although they desired to have children, their arms had remained empty. After seven long years, they decided to adopt their first baby. This seemed to end a season of grief and brought happiness to their world. Not long after, they adopted another child—a toddler who had been in foster care. Now in their forties, and adoptive parents to a boy of ten and a girl of eleven, Ralph and Muriel's family was complete.

When Evaline suggested they adopt another child, Muriel's response was firm. "I couldn't possibly do it," she replied. But Ralph wasn't so quick to dismiss the idea. For years he had been quietly wondering whether they might one day add another little one to their family. It had been over ten years since their first adoption, but at lunch that day, the helper's request stirred something within them both. Perhaps it was a sense of obligation—after all, this was a young Christian woman in trouble, and they had the ability to help. Whatever their motivation, a few weeks later Ralph and Muriel found themselves making the drive to Auckland, where the papers were signed and I was handed over to my new parents.

༄♡༄

THE SECRECY AND SHAME surrounding unmarried pregnant women brought much heartache. In fact, between the 1950s-1980s, approximately 100,000 adoptions, most of them closed, occurred in New Zealand alone. My mother was one of many women who felt they had no option but to pursue adoption for their babies. There was typically no support available for the mother unless the wider family were willing to take in the baby, and this, along with the fact that so many married couples wanted to adopt at the time, made it the most obvious and helpful solution for all involved. Many girls in these circumstances were sent to homes for unmarried mothers, and while there are sadly some heartbreaking stories, there are also thankfully those who found mercy and kindness, depending on where they ended up. Some expectant women were sent to stay with a distant friend or extended family and were able to come back home—having given birth and placed their newborn for adoption—to try and pick up the pieces. Many women, however, chose to move somewhere completely new after going through such a life-changing experience.

A deep sense of sadness accompanies the separation of a mother and her newborn baby. For centuries it was thought that babies were effectively a 'blank slate' at birth and would therefore quickly adapt to their new parents and environment when placed with their adoptive families. This thinking, although long outdated, continued to linger in terms of adoption. In every other respect, it was well understood that bonding begins in the womb. During the pregnancy, the mother and baby are in tune with each other's rhythms, sounds, and even heartbeats, and this forms a strong attachment between them. Although it can present in different ways, it is now recognised that both mother and baby experience trauma and loss as a result of separation. Research has shown that our implicit memory retains feelings from even before birth, and that when attachment has been interrupted at an early age—particularly in pre-verbal infants—the sense of abandonment they experience can remain internalised for many years. This deep feeling of woundedness can threaten the child's sense of security and impact their lives well into adulthood.

The loss is felt by the mother too. Today, I feel genuine compassion towards my birth mother. Ostracised by some of her family and friends, the wounds ran deep. Soon after I was born, my birth mother moved to Australia. She had given me life and my first name, Sheri. She hoped for a fresh start and managed to make a new life for herself, leaving her past far behind her.

THE DAY I LEFT the hospital, I was taken by my new family to their home a few hours away—a house on a large property with lovely lawns and beautiful gardens. By all accounts I was very unsettled and cried for much of the time, so much so that my parents had to leave the vacuum cleaner running so I could fall asleep. This was not unusual, as many adopted babies proved difficult to settle, and signalled distress during their transition to living with a new family.

As was common during those years, mine was a closed adoption. Limited information was passed on, and neither party could contact the other, making the whole process very secretive. My new parents weren't given much background information—only a brief description saying my birth mother was intelligent and attractive, and that she had named me Sheri. As was the custom, my adopted family decided to rename me, and my new brother and sister were given the task. My brother chose Lynnette, and my sister chose Fay.

At that point, a new birth certificate was issued, and my original birth certificate containing the name of my birth parents as well as the name my mother had given me, was sealed and filed away as though none of us had existed before then. The legal system had done its job. It was as though they were saying, "Here's the baby. Go and live your life!" From that point forward, I was no longer Sheri but Lynnette Fay. I had been given a new name and a new family.

2

Am I Safe?

SOON AFTER I ARRIVED at my first real home, my adoptive parents moved to a new town about an hour and a half away. I remember little of it—apart from an incident that occurred when I was a toddler. This was before car seats and child restraints were required, and that day, as we were slowly driving along, I leaned on the door handle of the car and fell out onto the road below. The family stopped the car and rushed to my side. "Am I dead?" I asked, looking up at their concerned faces. That question became an ongoing family joke, but it was my first conscious memory, and despite the humour, it left me shaken.

I wonder now how much that incident played into some of my childhood insecurities. As far back as I can remember, a part of me has always questioned whether I was safe. Although I was certainly loved and cared for, I often felt uneasy. A sensation much like homesickness became familiar to me. Perhaps because my earliest life experiences were marked by loss, I lacked a sense of stability and wondered many times if and where I truly belonged.

Part of my uneasiness during that time was related to the house we lived in. Dad worked at the local dam, and our family's house was supplied with his job. The rooms had very little natural light, and I was glad when

Dad set to work raising the floor in the dining room so we could sit at the table and look out the window at the beautiful lake in the distance.

One day, Dad took me to work with him to watch the floodgates being opened. I stood holding his hand as water rushed over the causeway. It should have been a spectacular sight, but as the water crashed into the river below with a deafening noise, I was certain I was about to die. Seeing my terror, my dad took me inside the hydroelectric plant, however, the noise of the turbines tormented me even further. Although I was relieved and happy to return home that day to some sense of safety and security, I was left with a feeling of foreboding.

I found comfort in being at home with my family, but I also looked forward to the weekend when we would dress up in our Sunday best and go to church together. The hymns and readings conveyed something loving and secure, and I felt God's presence during the service. Some Sundays, Mum would play the organ or make a floral arrangement to display at the front of the church. But the most reassuring times were when I got to sit close beside my mother and hear her harmonise with the music. Perhaps something about the gentle words and calming music soothed my childhood heart—even if I did fall asleep during the readings.

Dad often said that I was a particularly tender, sensitive child. "I hardly ever had to tell you off," he told me later in life. "I only had to lower my voice and your lip would drop and quiver. How could I ever be harsh with you?" This certainly wasn't the case for my brother and sister, however. They were often disciplined, and whenever I overheard this happening I would take off to another room and hide, just to make sure I was safely out of the way.

As the family grew, making ends meet on Dad's income alone became challenging, and when I was four, we shifted again. Mum took on some part-time office work and kept busy making home-cooked meals and sewing our clothes on her well-used Husqvarna sewing machine. Our parents were both keen gardeners, and the veggie patch in our new backyard flourished. My mother encouraged us to be content. "You might not have everything you want, but you have everything you need," she often said. And although her words felt somewhat true, a sense of dissatisfaction was already niggling inside me.

We settled into our new home, and I started kindergarten, affectionately known as 'kindy'. I have fond memories of painting, playgrounds, little hooks I could reach to hang up my jacket or bag, and, most importantly, heartily singing along to vinyl records playing on turntables. My mother took me to kindy on her pushbike, peddling along at the front with me seated behind her on the back carrier. This was fine—until one day my foot slipped and became tangled in the back wheel spokes, resulting in many tears and a trip to the hospital. Perhaps this was the first time I remember feeling truly scared. Strangers kept wanting to check my foot, but they only made it more painful. The sights, sounds and smells of the hospital, along with being somewhere unusual once again, only increased my fearful feelings, and I was glad to go home again.

Eventually, I was able to return to kindy, and the part I looked forward to the most was the singing. One particular memory I have is of singing along to my favourite song, "My Bonnie Lies Over the Ocean," except I had the words mixed up and was actually singing at the top of my voice, "My *body* lies over the ocean!" As a little girl, I wondered about those strange words, but I loved the singing too much to let my lack of understanding put me off. Every time the red record player came out, I knew it was going to be the best part of the day.

When the time came for my fifth birthday, Mum made a special birthday cake. It was iced and decorated with little dolls dancing around a maypole with ribbons—a replica of the birthday cake my sister had when she turned five. The novelty was fun, and I especially liked having the same themed cake as my older sister. The sense of family connection, even at this young age, brought warmth to my heart and a feeling of belonging that I yearned for.

Turning five meant starting primary school. My first day involved a lot of tears as it required leaving Mum and learning to adapt to another new environment. Adopted children can often feel anxious about new situations, raising the question of whether they will fit in or be rejected. My heightened sensitivity brought daily challenges. I asked one of my uncles, "How long do I have to go to school for?" and when he light-heartedly replied, "You need to keep going until you turn fifteen," I was quite inconsolable—and shocked!

I figured out early on that if I did what I was told at school, and did it well, there was a chance of being rewarded with a small, gold star badge. These were much coveted by most of the children (except for the mischief-makers who did not have any inclination towards gold stars—an idea that was totally baffling to me). Realising that my behaviour came with a predictable outcome, I quickly decided to try my best to 'do things right', and I liked the positive results. I do, however, also remember a moment of incredulous disbelief when a teacher told me off for chatting too much in class, and threatened to take my gold star away from me for behaving that way! This was bad news indeed for a six or seven-year-old who was desperate to please everybody, and I think I felt the ground move under my feet. Such was my dismay that a devastating punishment like this was even possible!

It took me longer to settle into school than most of the other children, but I eventually found learning enjoyable. It had a rhythm to it, and the shiny new stationery was a highlight of each term. School began to feel like a place I could mostly figure out and feel part of, which was especially important for me.

When I was six years old, I had another stay in hospital—this time to have my tonsils removed. I tried to be brave, but whenever time my mother left, and I was alone, tears would pour down my cheeks. Nurses berated me when I cried, and told me I would have to stay there longer if my tears would not stop. Being in a strange place once again was overwhelming, and inwardly I trembled. I felt insecure and craved the safety of being at home with my family.

But home wasn't always a comfortable place to be.

FIVE YEARS BEFORE I was adopted, Dad had been in a serious accident. While working on a power line, he fell and broke his back. He was in hospital for a long time, and for the rest of his life he endured crippling pain. Prior to his accident, he was a strong man, but afterwards, he needed to adjust the kind of work that he did. Dad still wanted to be a good provider, but he worried about his income. He also felt unsure about where he fitted in at church, which was an important part of his life. Mum had been through tough times as well. When she was a young girl, the Napier earthquake ruined her home, and her family were forced to live outside in a makeshift shelter, with only a sheet for a roof. My mum was an intelligent woman, however. She was dux of her school, and she knew her Bible inside-out and back-to-front.

Having lived through the Depression, both of my parents were frugal. They had very traditional roles and did not always see each other's point of view. Dad felt insecure about Mum working and earning money. His upbringing had been harsh and now, as a father himself, he was prone to outbursts of anger, especially when my brother and sister pushed the boundaries. I was too young to know what those boundaries were, but I observed and heard enough to know that it was better for me to keep quiet and stay out of the way. I felt I barely knew my siblings, but looking back, perhaps they intentionally made themselves scarce, not wanting to set things off at home.

Throughout my childhood, I enjoyed occasionally staying with a precious aunt and uncle who lived on a nearby farm. Their home felt safe and loving, and while their four children were at school, I would often follow my aunty around like a little shadow, collecting eggs from the chickens and participating in various daily rhythms that were both wholesome and fun. Their family was tangibly loving and supportive, and these were precious times. Conversations were open and warm, and I always felt welcome in their home. As bedtime approached, my nervous feelings would resurface. However, the first time I stayed there, I was both surprised and comforted to see a row of dolls and teddy bears lined up across the top of my bed to keep me company. Knowing I was unsure about so many things, they continued to pile on the reassurance as if they had a never-ending supply of loving-kindness. Music flowed through their home, and one of the many enjoyable things they were part of was being in a band called 'Simple Faith'. Even the name resonated with my heart.

Back at our family home, however, things were not so simple. Naturally sporty and creative, my brother could be both mischievous and serious. He had always been on the wild side—when he was only five, he ended up with serious burns from playing with matches and petrol with his friends. He spent many painful months in hospital before eventually coming home with a badly scarred leg. My parents took him to the beach where they said swimming in the ocean offered him the greatest healing. Still, it seemed my brother couldn't get away fast enough, and at the age of fifteen, when I was just five years old, he left to find work and live his own life

One night, after a particularly bad argument with Dad, my sister also left home. I heard raised voices, and as the situation escalated, I curled up into a ball inside a bedroom wardrobe. I hated hearing them fight, so I kept still and silent, trying to think about something else. For a long time, I felt guilty for hiding. *Should I have stopped them fighting? Had I somehow been part of the problem?* My mind frequently played tricks on me, and I often felt I was to blame for incidents unrelated to me. I was always on the lookout for things that might compromise my safety and found life confusing and hard to understand.

∾♡∾

MY RESPONSE TO BEING the only child left at home was to create an imaginary friend. I called her Linda. One day, while waiting in our parked car, I was having a very sincere conversation with Linda when someone walking past called out, "Hi, Linda," to a girl across the street. I spun around with such a look of shock and astonishment that someone else had a friend called Linda as well!

I also treasured having a pet to keep me company at home. One special black cat, Kimba, was my constant companion. Having trained him from a kitten, I could pop him in a small wooden nail box on the back carrier of my Raleigh 20 pushbike and ride all around the neighbourhood with him looking out over the side, his little white paws perched over the edge of the box. These were the best of times, and I understand how people can have such a close affinity with their pets as it eases loneliness. Each afternoon, Kimba would sit next to the mailbox on our driveway, waiting for me to come home from school, and I always looked forward to seeing him in his usual waiting spot. He was a loyal and lovely little friend and a delightful part of my childhood. This pattern continued for years until I came home one day to the sad news he had passed away. I cried and cried when our neighbour said he had found him in their garden, lying still and silent. It felt like I had lost a dear friend.

A lot of the time I lived in my own little world. I liked to play 'shops' though this was a little challenging, as I had to be both the customer and the shopkeeper. I enjoyed writing too, and I would tap away at my mother's manual typewriter pretending to write stories and make books. Another favourite pastime was tuning in to our small transistor radio and dancing around to the music. When I was seven, I joined the school choir. The kind-hearted tutor, clearly seeing my enjoyment, said, "While you are in my choir I will call you *Linnet*, because you are a little songbird." I felt like I grew a little taller in that moment. Other people's kind comments did more for me than they probably realised.

Because I was fond of music, I soon started piano lessons. On reflection, this must have been a luxury my parents could hardly afford. Lessons were held at the home of the music teacher, who was very abrupt and strict. This was yet another time when I felt anxious, and I worried about getting into trouble if my posture wasn't exactly right or I didn't hold my hands in the proper placement. When I was required to perform in front of an actual audience at the end of the year, I was so nervous—in fact, I even wanted to stop learning music because of the panic I felt.

As I waited to play my chosen piece of music in front of everyone, I was trembling inside. My heart was thumping so hard and my knees were shaking so much that I wasn't even sure if I could walk up to the piano. Thankfully, being one of the youngest to perform meant I didn't have to wait long for my turn, and despite feeling sick and frightened, I managed to appear outwardly calm, place my fingers in the right place, and play the tune. When I returned to my seat, it took a while to notice the other performances, but gradually the overwhelm subsided and I was greatly relieved it was over. After a couple of years, I began taking lessons with a younger music teacher who lived close by, and I could ride my bike there easily. She taught more contemporary songs, and her class was more light-hearted and fun. I felt more relaxed with her, and I also experienced a little confidence lift as my piano playing improved.

One area I quickly realised I was not going to excel at was gym class. When sports teams were being chosen, I was far from the first pick—it seemed like I had two left feet, and coordination was not my strong point. It was a steep learning curve as I was desperate to fit in, and my thoughts were never far from the risk of rejection in any situation. Once, when playing netball at primary school, the principal (of all people) told my mother, "It is just as well she has a good brain because sports are surely not her thing." As someone who was already aware of my shortcomings, it was not a particularly helpful or encouraging comment to hear. However, I learned to live with it even if I did feel like an outsider in those moments. "You can't be good at everything," my parents would say, but I really wished I could be.

The following year, while my class was looking forward to school camp, I felt terror at the thought of staying away from home. When we arrived, the dark rooms, odd musty smells, stories from the principal about taniwha monsters and odd occurrences all compounded my feelings of unease. I felt small and apprehensive, but though I craved reassurance, I was unsure of who to ask. During times like these, I prayed, believing God was watching over me. It was the only thing I knew to do, and without it, I would have crumbled. At camp, we went on bush walks and explored beautiful things in nature, but I could not understand why everyone else enjoyed the adventures. To me, it all spelt R-I-S-K. This is the reality for many adopted children, but it wasn't until later in life that I understood the fight, flight, freeze or fawn responses that had marked my childhood years and the stress I often felt I had to navigate.

❧♡❧

I WAS FOND OF WATCHING wholesome shows like *Lassie* or *Swiss Family Robinson* on television. Much to my sister's annoyance, the storylines frequently brought me to tears, but I loved a happy ending because it made me feel like, perhaps, everything *could* be right in the world. It wasn't that things were *wrong* in my life exactly, but somewhere deep inside, I just didn't feel like I was in the right place. It was a feeling I could not describe, nor could I even really accept that I felt that way.

I can't recall being told I was adopted, but it was never hidden from me. Nevertheless, the fact that I was adopted was always kept within the family. Whenever I asked my parents for more information about the day they adopted me, or about my first family, they would always give me a brief outline of what they knew. My mother noticed that I easily related to stories like *Pollyanna, The Sound of Music,* and *Anne of Green Gables* in which children had either lost their parents or were being raised in another family. Sometimes, I would even sleep with my long hair wrapped around rags, so I would wake up in the morning with curly hair like Pollyanna. When *The Sound of Music* movie was released, it was thrilling to go and see it at the cinema with my mum and sister. It was one of the rare occasions when it was just the three of us together, and I felt like I was walking on air. It is still my most-loved movie of all time.

When I was around nine years old, I went by myself to stay with Mrs. McPherson—a close family friend. We would typically enjoy sewing together and going to the movies, or I'd meet up with other children. One day, out of the blue, she made a comment that pierced my heart, "That's because you're adopted." I spun around immediately to see who else might have heard. My first thought was, *How does she know?* followed quickly by, *Who else knows?*

I vividly recall the shock of that moment. Suddenly, being adopted didn't feel like a special thing, but rather it confirmed I had something to be embarrassed about, something I didn't want others to know. From that day forward, it dawned on me that I didn't only have parents who had chosen me, but I had another mother somewhere out there and I longed to find her. The problem was, I had no idea who or where she was.

AFTER SHE MOVED OUT, my sister and I didn't see each other often, so it was a surprise when she asked me one day to be her rowing team's substitute cox in their eight-person boat. This was both exhilarating and terrifying, but I listened carefully to the instructions and gave it my best shot. It happened only once, but being invited to join the team gave me a huge boost and the feeling of being accepted—with the added bonus of spending time out on the water alongside my sister.

On two occasions, my sister and I were part of wedding parties as bridesmaids and flower girls. It felt extremely special to be able to share in the experiences with her. The first time, we dressed up in pink dresses with little white daisies imprinted on a sheer overlay. The dresses looked like they came from a fairy tale, and for a whole day, I felt like a princess. Looking back, I am sure our mother must have sewn our dresses. She was an extremely skilled dressmaker, and I'm sure it wasn't until I was around ten years of age that I got my first store-bought dress, a crisp white frock with country garden flowers all over it and a little capped sleeve with ruffles. The other wedding was our cousin's and again, I smiled throughout the entire day. Perhaps it was the joy of being exquisitely dressed with my hair done, or the closeness and connection with my sister, or maybe it was the flowers and beauty of the day that touched my young heart, but the occasion brought me a lot of happiness and is forever etched in my memory.

The next time I got to dress up was for the leaving dance at the end of my final year of primary school. My parents disapproved of dancing and discos, but to my great surprise, after a lot of pleading, they finally allowed me to go. Until this point, most of my friends were from church, the music I listened to was confined to a few songs on my transistor radio, and my life had been fairly sheltered. *Perhaps now it was time to push some boundaries of my own and learn to stretch my wings?*

3

Stuck in the Middle

My world was widening, and the start of intermediate school brought with it even more change. I'd gone from being a shy little girl in a confined world to wanting to explore more of my surroundings and make some of my own decisions.

Biking from the other side of our town to my new school was a big adventure in itself, but a positive one. I now had the opportunity to explore different subjects, and I found I especially enjoyed the practical classes, like cooking, woodwork, art, metalwork, and sewing. But my best subject was English. I did writing projects galore, and somehow I was able to find the information required—and add a million embellishments! This was certainly fun for me, though I'm unsure how the teachers felt about it! Then there was the marvellous moment when my grades would come in, and again I would feel taller than I truly was.

A simple but new experience was ordering lunch (if you could afford it), and choosing something from the lunch menu was a rare but special treat. Another positive was being part of the choir; we sang contemporary songs and once performed on stage in front of the entire school. Despite my nervousness, I somehow enjoyed singing ABBA's 'SOS' along with the rest of the group and lived to tell the tale.

The thought of standing out still made me very uncomfortable, and by now I was putting in great effort to fit in and cope with new situations. Thankfully, caring souls can sometimes come alongside us on our journey and offer life-giving support, and one such lovely person came into mine. One weekend, my brother brought his girlfriend home to meet our parents. I was a keen observer of people and situations, scoping out what and who was safe or otherwise, and after observing her for a while, it was clear that my brother had an angel for a girlfriend! She was twenty years old, but she happily slept in the same bedroom as me, and in the morning, she let me hop in her bed where we had great chats as if we were best friends. To my eight-year-old mind, this was the ultimate compliment! *Why would she be so kind and willing to open her beautiful heart to me?* Over time, I came to my senses and realised it was purely because she was one of the loveliest people in the world! I treasured being with her and, over time, was inspired to be like her. *She is a gem*, I thought, *and everyone loves her.* She instilled a sense of beauty and hope into a vulnerable season of my life, and when she married my brother and became part of our family, I was over the moon. It was an important lesson to never underestimate the power of being kind and loving to another person—for me, in that particular season, it was life-changing.

To make friends and encourage greater church connection, I went to Every Girls Rally—a girls' group at my church where we played games, earned badges, learned life skills, and heard Bible stories. It was good for a while, but after a few years, I began to outgrow it. In fact, I felt so unhappy about going that I ended up having a meltdown to my parents over it. I'm sure they wondered what on earth was happening, as I was normally so compliant. My default was to downplay and repress my opinions to avoid confrontation as much as possible.

Mum kept trying to encourage me to get to know a girl in the group whose parents were friends of hers, but I just wasn't comfortable with it. It was the first time I'd put my foot down and made my feelings clear, and later on, I realised these feelings were stirrings of God's guidance and protection. Once, when I had to stay with them, I stayed awake all night. I couldn't put my finger on what the trouble was, but I felt nauseous and restricted, and this strange discomfort put me on high alert. Eventually, I heard about unusual stories which confirmed my troubling feelings, and I learned to trust my intuition, even though it was confusing at times. This leads me to encourage any dear readers that if you ever feel uncomfortable about a place or a person, please be brave and tell someone about it. It is important to feel safe and to be seen and heard. I spoke up, and although the response at the time was disbelieving, I learned that it is always good to trust the intuition we have because there is often something valid behind it.

My prayers for protection were answered during that time; however, these uncomfortable situations led me to promise myself that if someday I had my own family, I would do my utmost to show my children that they were heard and seen, loved and lovely. It was a thought I repeated over and over to myself until it became a heartfelt vow.

THE PRETEEN YEARS ARE often a complex stage of life, and for me, this was heightened when my friends spoke about their families. Some clearly felt close to their parents, siblings, and extended families, while others seemed constantly frustrated or misunderstood at home. I noticed one thing, however, that left me feeling like something was missing in my story. Many friends expressed how they felt when they were compared to other family members. Sometimes this was positive, and other times it was a source of annoyance. "Everyone says I'm like so-and-so," they would say. While I understood what they meant, I realised no one had ever said that about me. *Who was I like?* Not my mum, particularly, or my dad. Not my brother or sister. And certainly not any extended family members. I loved them all, but the familial likenesses that my friends talked about just weren't there.

I found my thoughts often turning to my biological family. *Who were my people?* I wondered if I had siblings and if I resembled them in any way. *Did anyone have similarities to me in mannerisms or appearance? Where did my brown eyes come from? Were there talents somewhere in my ancestry that might be passed down the family line to me? Was my personality like anyone else's?* During this time, a great many questions were swirling around my brain concerning my core identity.

It was in the classroom, however, where the differences between me and most of my friends seemed most intense. Once my classmates knew I was adopted, there was no hiding from that reality. This caused particular problems when we were given 'family tree' projects. These seemed to come around every few years, perhaps because each new teacher wanted to get to know the students in their class. Whenever they mentioned family trees, I felt my stomach churn as if to say, *Not this again!* I remember feeling my face get hotter and hotter at the thought of what was to come.

I didn't know anyone else who was adopted, except for my older sister and brother, so I typically felt embarrassed when anyone brought it up and felt like I was the odd one out. As much as I tried to feel normal about not knowing my heritage, there was still an uneasy feeling about the lack of information I had been given. Sometimes people would say hurtful words like, "At least *my* mother loved me," trying to imply that being adopted meant you weren't loved. Yes, I had been raised by a couple who weren't my natural mother and father, but it is possible to be loved in the many different configurations that make up a family.

When my peers asked questions like "Who are your *real* parents?" I would flinch. *What does 'real' parents even mean?* I wondered. I had parents—my mum and dad—and they were certainly real, but I also knew that, just like everyone else, I had a mother and father who were my biological parents. *Did the fact that I was adopted make me any less real?* I began to wonder. *Who was the real me?* Suddenly, my whole identity seemed up for debate.

Outwardly, I was generally happy, but inwardly I wrestled against an undercurrent of confusing thoughts that were always close to surfacing. I found myself easily startled, untrusting of others, and, in my more reflective moments, wondering if I should even be in this world. Exploring these thoughts was like pulling on a loose thread—everything would quickly unravel, and I'd find myself questioning, *How can I ever know what is actually true?* At times I would feel lost, but my faith was typically the anchor that steadied me.

❧♡❧

BEING PART OF A church gave me a feeling of community, but as the teen years approached, more and more questions popped up. I remember there was one lesson about loving others as you love yourself. I was on board with that concept, but when I was asked, "What does it mean to love your neighbour like yourself?" I found myself wondering, *How do we love ourselves?* I thought about it for a long time, with my heart thumping, before I finally plucked up the courage to ask it out loud. Unfortunately, an older gentleman in the church who was teaching us that day reprimanded me for asking the question. "Oh, don't be so silly. Of course you know what it means to love yourself!" Perhaps it was because I was a girl asking a question, or maybe he mistook me for being cheeky and challenging his comments. In any case, his response made me keep quiet about the topic, though inwardly those feelings and questions wouldn't go away. *Am I accepted by God?* I wondered. *Can I trust Him? Is the fact He is called 'Father' something I can cling to?*

If I do something wrong, will that make Him angry? Would I no longer be accepted by Him?

I knew there was nothing I could have done to make my biological parents keep me—after all, I was only a newborn. But now I was older and felt responsible for holding all my relationships together. *If my adopted family could choose me, perhaps they could un-choose me too,* I thought. If that was indeed the case, it all came down to pleasing them—my friends, family, siblings . . . even God. Subsequently, I was aware of always trying to be a 'good girl' and avoiding making any ripples or trouble. I often had difficulty believing that I measured up, even when I had good grades or was given compliments, I found myself second-guessing if I was good enough or if I was too much trouble. At times, I was surrounded by a sense of guilt and wondered if I was to blame for the things happening around me. I realised that all through my childhood I had felt pressure to do the right thing in order to keep God and those near to me onside. Quietly, I thought and prayed about these feelings, and although these thoughts would continually return, I felt that God understood my heart.

Now that I was in my teens, there was something about church that kept drawing me like a young plant towards the light. The warmth of familiar hymns and Bible readings seeped into my soul and nurtured my simple faith. When I was younger, I asked Jesus into my heart countless times just to make sure I was safely part of His family. The constant theme that ran through my thoughts and heart was that God was love, and He loved me. This belief was both a refuge and a great comfort throughout my life, soothing my longing for security and identity. Where there were wounds from all the disruption I had experienced in my early years, somehow His loving reassurance brought some healing.

Although this vertical relationship between me and God was getting firmer, my horizontal relationships were becoming more confusing all the time. I may have been growing in curiosity, but more than anything, I wanted to remain invisible.

IN MY MID-TEENS, IT was hard to tell how much of what I felt was simply being a teenager, and how much was the result of being adopted. When I was given opportunities, often I would not be able to go through with them. The underlying fears of my early childhood hadn't diminished— if anything, they had a tighter grip on me. Over time, however, my confidence grew incrementally. I loved fashion and enjoyed the creativity that went along with it. It was satisfying sewing my own clothes and wearing the finished pieces or hanging them in my wardrobe.

In sewing class at school, my teacher invited me to take part in an upcoming Young Fashion Designer competition. We could choose fabric and patterns and design two outfits for different sections. I sensed my parents had a lot to deal with at the time, and I hated the idea of loading my needs onto them, but thankfully, Mum gave her permission *and* let me choose the materials. When the time came to model the clothes, however, I couldn't muster enough courage or confidence to participate in the show. The clothes were made, but I was filled with overwhelming self-doubt, and at the last minute I backed out. Even the awful guilt I felt at the thought of the extra money my mother had spent on me was not enough to convince me to take the plunge and compete. It was a familiar pattern—if there was risk involved, a protective wall would go up and I would retreat. Many years later, I figured out the risk of failing was too immense for my young self to bear, and I finally forgave myself for being (what I thought was) a disappointment.

Church had been a constant throughout my childhood, and there was a feeling of fun and freedom being with similar-aged teens at youth group. Everyone began to call me Lynne, and it seemed like this came with a renewed sense of identity. I noticed, however, that there were differences between how our family interacted compared to some of the others. My parents didn't see eye to eye on many things, while other families seemed genuinely happy. When I observed these differences, I wondered if I was the cause of my parents' disharmony. The thought circled in my mind: *If I'm to blame, why am I even in this family?* This ultimately raised another question: *Should I even be here at all?*

Still, despite this inner confusion, I understood I was lucky to have a home and family, and I believed the fewer waves I made about anything, the better off everyone would be—including me. Little did I know that I was about to have a conversation that would unleash a tidal wave and change the landscape of my family forever.

4

Asking Questions

EVERYTHING CHANGED THE DAY my dad's sisters came to visit. We were all sitting around the dining table in the kitchen when one of my aunties blurted out to my sister, "So what was it like finding your birth mother?"

Things became suddenly tense, and I noticed a look cross Mum and Dad's faces as they glanced at each other and then at me. "Lynnette wasn't meant to hear that," Mum said, but it was too late. My mind was already racing.

What?! How could I not have known my sister had been looking for her birth mother, let alone met her?! And if I hadn't known about that, how many other secrets are being kept from me? If adoption is meant to be something good, why is there so much secrecy?

I stayed as still and quiet as I could, wanting to downplay the moment so they'd all keep talking. Inwardly, I was on high alert, hoping to hear as many details as possible. My sister shared in a matter-of-fact way that she had finally met her birth mum, but the conversation was short and brief, and the topic moved on quickly. For me, however, the cat was out of the bag. My mind and heart went to a million different places all at once. *Why had I been left out of such an important moment in my sister's life? Didn't they realise that I was just as adopted as my sister was?* I felt invisible in that moment. They must have known I'd be interested. At first, I felt frustrated that this had been kept from me, and then I felt annoyed. Even when a pet is adopted, it seems like more information is available than what I'd been given.

Then my curiosity kicked in. I'd often dreamed that one day I'd see my birth mother mysteriously on the street somewhere, but I'd never considered the possibility that I could actively look for her. Everything about our adoptions was shrouded in secrecy. *How had my sister done it?* Once I began considering the possibilities, I could not stop thinking about it.

Until now, my thoughts had often turned to questions about who my biological parents were and where they might be, but it was something I kept mainly to myself as the topic felt too big to bring up. When I was younger, I asked Mum repeatedly about what happened when they adopted me, and as she described their part of the journey, I would imagine the scene playing out in my mind. Over time, though, I became tentative about bringing it up as I sensed a sadness in her tone, and I didn't want to upset her. It felt like a prickly subject to talk about, and though I tried to be careful to avoid hurting my parents' feelings, I also desperately wanted to quell my curiosity and know for sure what my family tree was like before everything changed.

A part of me sensed a deep-rooted homesickness for my first family, an odd feeling of loss that simply would not go away. I felt like I always had a boot in two camps—one in my adopted family and one in my biological family whom I knew nothing about. The more I pondered the idea of searching for my birth parents, the more resolute I became. Still, I wanted the blessing of my parents before taking the next step. After hearing this new information about my sister's discovery, I sat with it for a few months before gathering the courage to broach the subject with my parents.

❧♡❧

IN THE MEANTIME, SOMEONE else had captured my imagination. I'd met Phil at church a year earlier, but since then he'd been away studying. Now he was home for the summer, and when our eyes met briefly at a wedding, my thoughts raced: *strong, sporty, sure of himself, goes to church, a solid guy*. When he smiled, it felt like the earth tilted and my heart skipped a beat. Phil continued his agricultural studies at Flock House training farm several hours away, but over time our paths increasingly crossed, and our friendship grew.

Phil and I were very different in many ways. He loved the outdoors and enjoyed sport, hunting and farm life, while I was a city girl at heart with a love for fashion, theatre, movies, and music. However, as we spent more and more time together, we realised we had our faith and a love of family in common, and from the start of our relationship, it felt 'right'. My dad used a saying in moments when he felt strongly about something but couldn't quite say what it was. "I just feel it in my bones," he'd say, and more often than not, he was right. I had the same feeling about Phil. For reasons I could never quite explain, I felt comfortable and safe with him. We saw things differently at times, but I knew I could trust him, and building a relationship with him was truly a happy time. Phil brought a sense of fun and adventure to my life, yet he cared for me too. Until now, I had often felt somewhat untethered or adrift, unsure of how or where I belonged, but with Phil at my side, I felt truly grounded and loved.

❧♡❧

THE MORE MY RELATIONSHIP with Phil developed, the more I pondered the possibility of finding my birth parents. Well-meaning folks tried to dissuade me with arguments like, "You don't know what you might find" and, "Isn't it better to just live your own life and not worry about that?"

They made remarks about being grateful and positive for the life I had now, and some even shared tales of adopted people they knew who had searched for their birth family only to end up disappointed or filled with regret. Their reactions triggered a surge of guilt and shame about my desire to find out more about my history, and I realised that very few people understood the yearning I felt to know where I came from.

Faced with this odd mix of reactions, I felt rather naughty, yet brave at the same time. For so long, I had wanted to "do the right thing and be a good girl." However, now I was about to make some headway, I was no longer dissuaded. Instead, I was drawn to finding out as many pieces as I could in the puzzle of who I was. *How could I ever go back to a life shrouded in unknowns when I realised there was now a chance of finding answers?* It wasn't that I was ungrateful, but for once, my need to find out more outweighed any potential risk. Most people wanted to know something about their ancestry or heritage. *Was it really so strange that I needed to find answers about mine?* Thankfully, there were many who encouraged and even urged me to keep going.

Eventually, I talked to my parents about wanting to know more about my origins. Choosing my time carefully, I bolstered the courage to explain my desire to find my birth mother, desperately hoping they would understand and not be upset. The last thing I wanted to do was hurt them in the process. To my relief, they understood and accepted my decision, almost as if they knew this day was coming. They suggested we start by contacting their friend who had asked them years ago if they would consider adopting another baby. This was a great place to begin. Evaline no longer worked at Childhaven, but my parents had kept in touch through Christmas cards and had her address. Together we composed a handwritten letter, explaining my desire to know more about my birth mother and asking if she had any information she could share. After feeling powerless for so many years, it felt good to take some solid action. A sense of exhilaration rose within me. Now there was nothing to do but wait for her reply.

I was overjoyed when an envelope arrived in our post box just a few weeks later. "Leave it with me," she wrote, "I'll get back to you soon." I couldn't wait to tell Phil. Picking up the phone, I could hardly contain my elation. The wheels were in motion! Phil was calm but excited for me and reassured me he would be there for me every step of the way. By now, he understood how important it was to me to find whatever answers were out there.

Evaline replied to our letter much sooner than I anticipated. In an unexpected turn of events, her response revealed something I'd never known—she and my birth mother were related. While she had been a helper at Childhaven, her niece—my birth mother—had fallen pregnant, and Evaline had taken it upon herself to find a home for the newborn baby. This information came as a great surprise! Until then, I'd presumed my adoption was random—as most were back then. I'd also assumed that because of the secrecy built into adoption law, there was no way to know who my parents were, let alone their whereabouts. It felt like we'd just short-circuited the entire process!

The letter didn't mention my birth father, but for the first time in my life I learned that my birth mother's name was Sandra, and I kept rolling it around in my mind, storing it and letting it settle into my memory. Although she had lived overseas for many years, she had recently returned to New Zealand. She was thirty-seven by now and had just got married and become a stepmother to four teenage children—three of whom had also been adopted. When our letter arrived, she was away on her honeymoon. Finding out that her aunty had received a letter from me and replied to it, 'set the cat among the pigeons' within their family. Some of my birth mother's sisters were apprehensive about what a reunion might mean for her, while others questioned the wisdom of even mentioning to her that I had sent a letter. For seventeen years, everyone in the family had strictly held the secret. Now, just as my birth mother's life was settling down, I had come back into the picture.

Evaline's response was measured. She finished her letter by saying that there were no secrets between Sandra and her new husband—he already knew that at the age of twenty, she had put her baby up for adoption—and yes, they would be happy to meet me. Evaline wrote that she had given my birth mother my phone number, and she would give me a call to work something out. I thought about what it must have been like for my birth mother to read that my name was now Lynne—not Sheri. *Was she, like me, realising that my name was just one of many details of my life that had changed over the years?*

I waited with bated breath for my mother to call. *How long would I have to wait? Would our conversation be strained, or easy? Would we naturally 'click'? What would it be like to finally be able to talk to my first mother?!*

Later that week, the phone finally rang. My mother's voice was warm and breezy and friendly on the other end of the phone. She sounded happy to hear about how my life was going and said she was looking forward to meeting me soon. As we arranged a time and place to meet, our plans were tinged with nervous excitement. Joking about how we didn't even know what each other looked like—all I had been told was that my mother was attractive with long brown hair—we eventually decided, "Let's meet at the domain, by the second lamp-post near the furthest pond from the car park."

As I hung up from the call, my thoughts were going in every direction. *I'd heard her voice, but what did she look like? Would she resemble me in any way?* I'm sure the questions were piling up for both of us.

❧♡❧

WHEN THE DAY FINALLY came, Phil came and picked me up for the two-hour drive to Auckland. On the way, we speculated about what it would be like to meet the woman who had brought me into the world, whom I had wondered about for years. Underneath my excitement, I was a bundle of nerves. I had no idea what to expect or how I should feel. It was all very surreal. For so long I had felt some semblance of rejection. *Would she accept me for who I was?* I longed for our first meeting to go well.

The park was full of families picnicking and playing games—it was a lovely atmosphere. As we walked, Phil held my hand and reassured me everything would be alright, and I appreciated the sense of ease he carried. Sandra arrived with her new husband, and before long, we spotted each other a short distance away, each step bringing us closer together. My first mother and I had been apart since I was a few weeks old, yet it seemed very natural for us to reunite now. Recognising each other with warm smiles, we embraced. The two men quietly slipped off to the side to chat while we found a nearby place to sit and talk. I could hardly believe I was finally sitting with my mother. I had waited so long for this moment, and my head and heart were spinning all at once as I tried to process the joy I felt.

Sure enough, we shared similarities. We both had brown eyes, a familiar smile, and several likenesses that revealed we were kin. A sudden sense of groundedness came over me. I'm sure I must have stared at her, trying to sear her image into my mind. We sat there for a couple of hours, talking and listening, both wanting to know about each other's lives. Now and then we noticed ourselves making a similar gesture, and we laughed about how this could be since we'd spent most of our lives apart. It was clear as we tried to fill in the gaps and find ways to reassure each other that both of us wanted the other to be happy and not carry any regrets about the past.

My birth mother shared how the circumstances in the 1960s were so different to how they are today. She knew that her choices were virtually non-existent. Advised that adoption would offer the best outcome for all concerned, she could only hope that everything would work out. My heart ached with compassion for the burden she had carried and how tough it had been for her to handle such a big decision—and the heartbreak. She told me she had enquired about getting me back when I was six months old, but by then the adoption wheels were in motion, the process was already in the courts, and it was very difficult, if not impossible, to turn things around.

Since my birth mother's aunty was working at Childhaven, she had some influence regarding where I was placed for adoption. As we continued to talk, we were saddened by all the years spent keeping secrets. It was bewildering why everything had to be so private—and how much it had all changed. Realising how different the world was for my mother around the time I was born brought greater understanding and healing, and I so valued the opportunity to start piecing the missing parts of my origin story together.

When I asked about my biological father, her face dropped as if she was drawn back into the sadness of that time. She communicated one thing very clearly: my birth father wasn't at all interested, and that she had been deeply hurt by the whole ordeal. She had, however, kept one solitary photo of him which she handed to me to keep. Although I wanted to know as much as possible, I didn't want to push her further. This was clearly not the time to pry her about the one question I had been longing to know. She did tell me that I had blood-related siblings but that they were from my father, not her—and noticing it seemed painful for her to talk about, I left it at that. I was walking a tightrope trying to keep the conversation comfortable for us both, yet something inside me flinched at the idea that I had contributed to her pain.

Thankfully the moment of awkwardness was broken when her husband, overhearing the topic of conversation, piped up with, "You'll never believe this! Just the other day Sandra and I saw a car drive past with signwriting on the side. I turned to her and commented, 'I purchased our car from the guy who previously owned that company,' and she straightaway replied, 'No way! The guy who used to own that company is the father of the baby I adopted out!' We laughed when we realised that we had been driving around in your biological father's old car!"

Needless to say, Phil and I were wide-eyed at this coincidence—and rather amused by it as well. Quietly, I tucked the thought away that perhaps one day, when the time was right, I might be able to meet my biological father too. For now, that thought had to be put firmly on the back burner. Meeting my birth mother may not have been quite like it is often portrayed in television shows, but there was a happy contentment to the day.

As PHIL AND I drove home that evening, we talked all the way, unpacking every moment scene by scene. Knowing my birth mum's identity helped further consolidate my sense of who I was, and my heart was filled with gratitude. It was sad to hear about her experiences from back then, but I was thankful we could meet, as not everyone who searches for their biological family can find each other. We'd agreed to get together again in a few weeks so I could meet her mother and sisters.

It felt like a bolt of joy when Sandra introduced me to my grandmother and aunties. We had arranged to meet at a café, and afterwards, they asked if they could take me to the shop next door to buy me a dress. My seventeen-year-old heart skipped a beat as we realised we were all drawn to the same style. When I tried on the dress and stepped out of the changing room, there was unanimous agreement: This was the one! The approval etched on each person's face stayed with me long after that day.

I didn't know at the time, that this would be a one-off occasion. I never saw my grandmother again, and I only got together with my aunties very occasionally. But every time I wore the dress, I reminisced about that moment. It was the first thing we'd done together as a family, and it felt like acceptance. The missing pieces of my life were finally falling into place. And as the gaps were slowly being filled, I was beginning to feel more whole.

5

The Greatest of These is Love

FOR A WHILE, I basked in my newfound sense of belonging. My confidence had been bolstered too—a fact that was evident the day I blurted out an answer in a tutorial. I'd enrolled in a secretarial course at my local technical college, and that day I had a class in communication skills. The tutor was unpacking the theme of what makes people tick, when he asked a surprising question: "What is one thing we all need to survive?"

My usual caution vanished, and I had a burning desire to answer. My hand shot up in the air, and I confidently replied, "Love." Never had I been more sure about an answer. My reply, however, was met with an outburst of laughter from my tutor and classmates. *How had I come up with that?* Everyone else was thinking food, water, a roof over your head . . . My cheeks blushed bright red. Yet in that moment, I felt I had uncovered the meaning of life!

For years I had struggled to understand who I was and where I belonged. Finding the maternal side of my family tree had satisfied part of my longing for acceptance and helped to assemble some of the fragmented pieces of my heart. But although we felt a sense of endearment toward each other, I was beginning to see that connecting with my birth mother and family after all this time could not replace or 'fix' the lost years we had spent apart. I still struggled with feelings of low self-worth as long-held insecurities resurfaced. For as long as I could remember, my head told me I was loved, but somehow, I grappled to believe it.

I remember people saying, "At least you weren't aborted" or, "Well it's just good that you're here." Of course I was grateful to be alive, yet those comments also invalidated my insecurities and skirted over the questions I and many adopted children faced. My default response was to shift the blame to myself, questioning my legitimacy once more. Unable to simply replace my core feelings with gratitude, I couldn't help but wonder if something was broken in me, whether the adoption was somehow my fault, and if I was ultimately unlovable.

Learning to feel loved was a slow burn, and it took years to feel confident in that. Instinctively, I knew God was love, and this was something I held on to. I wondered if everyone felt this curiosity about love or if it was an echo that resounded from the very beginnings of my life. I knew that maternal separation at infancy could result in long-term effects on a child's ability to feel loved, but part of me felt this was too big a topic to delve into. *Wasn't I supposed to have enough faith to quell those feelings?* Even so, I felt the tension of holding onto God's love, while also longing to feel secure and safe and loved by another.

I was uncertain about many things, but over time, as our friendship grew, I realised I felt safe and loved when I was with Phil. With him, my shaky sense of trust found solid ground, and he had a sense of fun that felt like fresh air. I could talk to him about anything, and when my insecurities rose, he was always reassuring, making me feel seen and heard. I was starry-eyed around him and always looked forward to spending time together, but I could tell some families in our church were surprised to see us together. Older friends gave me well-meaning advice about how this relationship would probably not work out and questioned what I was thinking. "You're so young, it would be silly to think this will lead anywhere," they said. "You're into such different things, how could it ever work?" I tried desperately not to take these words to heart—in fact, deep down I dared to believe there might be a glimmer of hope that one day he would ask me to marry him, so I prayed.

For such a momentous event, the proposal was a simple scene. Dropping me home after a night out together, Phil leaned over in the car and asked me to marry him. I was overjoyed and had no hesitation in saying yes. Phil hadn't yet asked my parents' permission, so I held off telling anybody right away, but when I went to bed that night, I could hardly sleep. It seemed like a miracle. My dream was coming true.

The following night, Phil came to dinner. I was fidgety with anticipation as I waited for him to say something to my parents. Finally, when the plates were cleared away and we were about to have dessert, Phil leaned on the table and said, "The main reason I've come tonight is to ask if I can marry Lynne." I knew my parents would be more than happy with the match, and sure enough, Mum let out a happy exclamation, while Dad nearly fell off his chair. Recovering quickly, he blurted out, "Oh no, I've got to do another speech!" and we all laughed. "So, is that a yes?" Phil asked. With everyone in hearty agreement, we went about setting a wedding date for five months' time.

Later that night, Dad mentioned another reason he was surprised. "We thought you might have waited a bit longer, seeing as you're still so young. But we couldn't think of a better person for you to marry." I was delighted. Summer would soon be here, and in the meantime, there was plenty to keep us busy.

My birth mother was pleased to hear our news, and our friends were thrilled for us, although a few were surprised at the match. I remember one friend laughing heartily when he noticed a muddy pair of rugby boots and a glossy bridal magazine lying next to each other on the back seat of Phil's car. These two incongruous objects perfectly captured our relationship. Phil was rugged and earthy while I was always trying to be 'put together'. For me, however, it seemed a perfectly natural fit. Our two worlds were coming together.

PLANNING OUR WEDDING BROUGHT my parents and me closer together. It was reassuring to have my mum and dad gather around me in such practical ways, but I also sensed some relief in them—as though any sense of obligation they had felt while raising me had been fulfilled now that Phil and I were preparing to launch a family of our own. I had found a place in their hearts, and now they were ready to let me go.

At the tender age of eighteen, I was very happy to be marrying my best friend and knew that somehow God had brought this man into my life. But as we considered how to merge my biological and adopted families, the question of who to invite to the wedding brought with it some complexities. I was once again trying to find a happy balance in navigating these sensitive issues without wanting to hurt anyone's feelings. I was grateful that my parents kindly invited my birth mother and her husband to join us for our wedding day.

The morning of our wedding, I felt nostalgic. Ours was a modest home but my parents had tended the garden especially for this day, and it looked beautiful. They had worked hard to bring the day together even though financially it was a strain for them, and while I appreciated this more as the years passed, I was struck by their kindness towards Phil and me as we made the transition into married life.

Dad and I travelled together to the church. There was a closeness between this private, shy man and myself. As I sat next to him in the wedding car, several fond moments we had shared from my childhood surfaced—a picnic we shared beside a nearby stream, a trip to the pools on a hot summer's day and him treating me to an ice cream soda . . . I could tell from the little half-smile on his face that he was nervous, so I placed my hand gently on his, letting him know everything was alright.

When we arrived at the church, Dad seemed anxious and shy about walking me up the aisle, but as soon as the music started he found the strength and we made our way to the front of the church behind our bridesmaids and our flower girls in their pretty pink dresses.

My dad stood there silently when the pastor asked the traditional question, "Who gives this woman to this man?" but with a little nudge from me he quickly responded, and we were all smiling as I joined my groom at the front. Phil was proud and teary-eyed. "You look beautiful," he whispered, and my heart nearly burst. After welcoming the guests, the pastor read a passage about the nature of love from 1 Corinthians 13, and before we knew it, it was time to exchange our vows.

Nothing could have prepared me for what came next. Hearing the words, "I Phil, take you, Lynne . . ." negated any doubt about my identity. I was Lynne, and Phil had chosen me! Suddenly, a great sense of belonging came over me. Contrary to any past thoughts, I *was* supposed to be here, in this world, at this time, in this place.

Our wedding day was the best day of my life up to that point, and throughout the festivities, there was an overwhelming feeling of connectedness and joy.

My birth mother and her husband came to our wedding, and later, when the photographer was at the park capturing our wedding photos, he took a discreet photo of the four of us, rather than at the church with everyone crowding around. They appreciated being included, but adoption reunions were still not common at that time, and we were all figuring out how to manage each step as it came up. Some of the guests were asking questions, and it took a lot of courage for Sandra to come. I was pleased they could join us, and grateful for Mum and Dad's willingness to have open minds and hearts towards them. When they met my birth mother, everyone acted rather shy and tentative towards each other, realising the uniqueness of the situation. There was a humble feeling of gratitude, and my parents thanked her for sharing me with them.

Craving harmony, I was thankful for their reactions—though I still felt a little torn as I tried to show allegiance to my parents as well as my birth mother. Reuniting meant picking up threads from long ago and attempting to weave them back into the tapestry of our lives. Feeling unsure of how to tie in these changing dynamics naturally and navigate this unknown territory without hurting anyone, turned out to be a new challenge. Adoption was part of my story but it was not my entire story. My birth mother and I had missed out on large parts of each other's lives, and reuniting felt like trying to build a bridge over a great chasm. We were relieved to finally know each other, but we both struggled to figure out where and how we fit in our present-day lives.

Following afternoon tea, Phil and I thanked our parents and said our goodbyes. I gave my wedding bouquet to my birth mother as a heartfelt gesture to thank her for coming. Then, we made a run for it. My brother caught sight of us trying to make a quick escape and darted through our neighbour's back lawn, ready to trip us up. But we managed to slip away to where our car was hidden and made a hasty getaway to the airport. The following day we would join a cruise around the Pacific Islands and begin the rest of our lives.

OUR LIFE TOGETHER WAS town and country as Phil worked on the dairy farm and I headed off every morning to my secretarial job. We enjoyed setting up the quaint old farmhouse together, and you could say our style was minimalistic before it became fashionable as we didn't have a lot. Sharing my life with someone was wonderful, and I felt less and less like a foreigner in the world. But like any couple, we had to learn how to accommodate each other. While Phil was used to sports, outdoors, and adventure, I was more accustomed to a quiet, sedate environment. He was happy to go hunting, whereas my interests were more homely. I remember making myself busy choosing curtains and rearranging furniture. All the while, little field mice tried to find their way inside the house, resulting in a shrieking wife! We were slowly learning how to compromise and take each other's likes and dislikes into consideration, but it was all part of the journey of getting to know one another more intimately. My sense of identity became more stable in my role as Phil's wife. He helped me find a firm foundation, and he says I, in turn, helped soften his heart.

Farm life brought with it several surprises—including the unwelcome arrival of severe hay fever. As I optimistically learned how to drive a tractor and mow hay paddocks, rivers of tears streamed down my face, and I couldn't stop sneezing. Then there was the time I chased a poor cow to the end of the farm in an attempt to bring her back to the cowshed—it takes a while to figure these things out! The first time I witnessed a rabbit being killed by our farm dog, I promptly burst into tears and needed convincing that this was a normal part of farming life. There were so many things to get used to, even down to figuring out that if Phil had to work late on the farm and dinner was ruined, it wasn't the catastrophe I thought it was. Sometimes old insecurities would rise and I would be unexpectedly triggered, but all of these new changes brought growth and a new sense of purpose as we faced the ups and downs of life together.

At times, I was genuinely surprised by the changes that were happening within me. A friend called in one day, and presumably because there was now a wife in the house, he promptly made himself comfortable and asked me to make a cup of tea. My response, "Well you certainly know where the jug and teapot are!" provoked a rather surprised look as I had always tended to keep these kinds of thoughts to myself. This new confidence was liberating, and I was no longer content to comply just to keep everyone happy.

Gradually, the haunting question of whether I was unlovable diminished. I remember coming home from work one day and noticing the words, "I love you" mown into the thick grass of our lawn and realising that layer by layer, my heart was healing. It was certainly an adjustment for a town girl like me to live in such a rural setting, but I treasured not feeling alone anymore. I was in love and couldn't think of a single other place on the planet I'd rather be than at Phil's side. For the first time in my life, I felt at home.

6

A New Start

PHIL AND I WERE excited to start our own family and sure enough, within a few months, I found out I was pregnant. I loved preparing and nesting, and spent hours hand knitting a woollen shawl that we would wrap our babies in. These were healing times, and I cherished the thought of becoming a mother.

The discomfort of my background motivated me as we began this new branch of our family tree. I relished the opportunity to make good on my earlier promise to myself to ensure my children felt heard and seen, loved and lovely. I was determined to make things lovely at home—not only by prettying up the room for the new baby but by setting a tone, along with Phil, of warmth and safety and love. More than anything, I wanted the heart of our home to be healthy.

What a joyous day (and night and day) it was when our first baby came along! Yes, the labour seemed to go on for days, and I wondered if I was going to make it through, but finally, our first daughter was born just as dawn was arriving. When we laid eyes on her everything else in the world drifted off into pale fog. As we embraced our precious baby girl for the first time, I knew she was the ultimate gift. My heart was so full of wonder as I held her in my arms. Phil could hardly bring himself to leave the hospital as he was so very fond of holding her, and the feeling was obviously mutual, as she slept soundly and rested in his strong arms. We were mesmerised by this new miracle and felt that *surely* no one had ever felt like this after having their first baby. The nurse told us later she had never seen a couple and new baby look so happy together. She may have said this to all the new parents but since we were so overjoyed, who was I to argue? Our parents and extended families couldn't wait to meet their newest grandchild, and as I watched them cuddle her with looks of love and endearment, my heart swelled with joy. As we gazed upon our firstborn child, it was like all the stars and planets had aligned. We were so very thankful for her—and I was surprised by how naturally we bonded. We were inseparable.

Phil and I flourished with our family of three. Like most new parents, we enjoyed taking lots of photos of our newborn, and I considered how my baby photos started only after my adoption at eight weeks. I couldn't help but reflect on how my birth mother might have felt when I was born. Her circumstances were so different from mine; there were no celebrations that day. *Was anyone happy for her when I was born? Did her family come to witness my arrival into the world and welcome me?* It was hard to imagine, and my sorrow for that scene, in such contrast to our own, felt heavy. I pictured my mum holding me, the newborn her womb had nurtured for months, knowing that we had to be separated. These fresh insights grieved me. Pondering her heartbreaking trials and loss made me acutely aware of how my adoption must have affected our attachment during those early weeks of my life.

I had told my birth mother that she was welcome whenever she wanted to visit, and just a few weeks later, she and her husband came to our home to be introduced to the newest member of the family. We captured this special milestone in all our lives with a photo of the three generations together—my first mother, my baby girl, and me. It was a lovely moment, though tinged with the awareness that this baby was, in a sense, an extension of my biological family, yet also disconnected. We treasured such moments, but mostly we navigated our day-to-day life as a little family of three, and we were content.

PHIL AND I LOVED our life together from the start, but we especially cherished our first year as parents. Still, I was unprepared for the wave of grief that crashed over me when, sixteen months later, we sadly experienced a miscarriage. It took me a long time to recover. My hormones were out of kilter, my emotions were raw, and thoughts of whether it was my fault came to the forefront again, even though our doctor reassured me I wasn't to blame. Once again, my foundations were rocked to the core as I grappled with a deep sense of loss and failure. I wanted to be safe and reliable, not powerless, but this was out of my control. My confidence dropped, and everything I held dear in my safe little family nest felt threatened. For the longest time, I had believed that I could keep my world safe and secure by 'doing things right' and not making mistakes. This was a situation where nothing I could have done would have changed the outcome, yet my heart could not accept this. Instead, I was filled with self-doubt and felt desperately in need of forgiveness.

Phil felt the loss keenly, and for a while I struggled with everyday tasks. But we held on to each other and our faith and found solace in being with our innocent little girl who was oblivious to the grief we were experiencing. Over time, I was able to come to terms with the fact that the miscarriage wasn't my fault and to pick myself back up from the heartache. It was Phil who steadied me through this time. I leaned on him, drawing a strength I didn't possess myself until eventually I came back to the firm foundational truth that I was loved . . . by him, and by God.

In the following years, we suffered another two heartbreaking miscarriages. But another lingering question frequently came to the surface: *Were my little lost babies safe and sound?* It was my father who helped settle the question. I was at my parents' home one day when my dad reassured me that our little babes were not lost but safe and sound in heaven. To this day, I find consolation in this.

To our great relief, a new baby son soon joined our family followed by another beautiful baby girl. We embraced being a family of five for several years before our fourth baby was born. Making his grand entrance on Valentine's Day, we fondly gave him the nickname 'Valentino'. A few hours after he was born, my midwife, a kindhearted woman of Māori heritage, came into the room and began sharing how important it is in her culture for all the siblings to bond with the baby as soon as possible. We felt the warmth and significance of her traditions and accepted them quite naturally. Later that afternoon, when she noticed our children trailing into the maternity ward to meet their new brother, she set up a warm bath for our new babe, gently placed him in the water and then invited our other three children to come and help wash him. With tentative, caring hands, they smiled as they welcomed him together. This moment touched me deeply as I realised the opportunity to bond with my siblings like this was not even an option for me early in life. It felt as though my own birth story was being redeemed with this new chapter, and I treasured these moments of love and acceptance.

Sixteen months later, not to be left out, our fifth child was born on a midwinter's day at dawn. Eager to make this early bonding experience a tradition, we followed the wisdom of our previous midwife and encouraged hands-on love from his siblings as soon as possible. There was never a shortage of open arms ready to cuddle their new baby brother. Bringing new life into our family was a team effort—I never had to question whether Phil would be there, he just always was. His authentic love was a blessing to me, and his solid, fatherly care towards our children has brought a constant sense of security and home.

The day finally came when we were able to buy our first home—a newly-renovated, cosy little bungalow right next to the river, just down the road from the dairy farm where Phil worked. It was only a little place, but it was filled with love. We took comfort in the fact that we were now a family of seven with a beautiful sense of belonging, community, and connectedness.

❧♡❧

THE DECADE AHEAD, HOWEVER, brought its share of changes—beginning when the farm where Phil worked was put up for sale. We took the opportunity to reassess our needs and decided it was time to leave dairy farming behind. As a family, we'd made wonderful memories in the coastal region about two hours away. It was an area rich in horticulture, and when a real estate agent showed us a kiwifruit orchard with plenty of grazing land that had just come onto the market, the possibilities captured our imagination. We looked forward to having a more manageable routine—one where we could be flexible rather than being tied by milking times, as it became more and more important to be involved with our family's activities as the children grew.

Mostly, our children were excited about the move, but for our eldest daughter, who had just started high school and made good friends, her emotions were understandably mixed. Still, when the moving truck left and we turned the key in the door for the last time, we were ready for our new venture.

Our new home needed renovations, but it was large, and with a little glimpse of the ocean in the distance, we could see this being a place to put down roots for our family for generations to come. When New Year's Eve rolled around that year, and with it the turn of the century, our hearts felt joyful and content. We were starting afresh, and once again we were surrounded by family and new friends. When our church heard we were hosting a New Year's party, they joined in the planning, and before we knew it, our bare paddocks were turned into race tracks, a flatbed truck became a stage for musicians, a huge screen created an outdoor movie theatre, and we soon lost track of how many people had come as everyone turned up with food and drinks to share, and brought their friends as well.

As I reflected on how all this had come about, I was a little bewildered. *How could it be that someone from such small beginnings had ended up with the opportunity to host an evening like this?* My life seemed to have taken a massive leap forward. It was a happy event, yet even in the celebrations, I still somehow felt like an observer rather than an active participant without fully understanding why.

I WAS THIRTY-SEVEN, AND still very much a learner in life. By now we had expanded our orchard, and the business side of things was a learning curve. The same was true on the family front. I loved being a mum, yet as the children grew older, I found myself constantly needing to grow and stretch. Determined to spend as much time together as we could, we'd often pack a picnic and head out together for a day of waterskiing and boating at some secluded bay at the lake, creating memories and trying to make sure everyone knew how much we loved them, even amidst a jam-packed life.

I was unprepared, however, when at the age of sixteen, our eldest daughter left home. For a year or so beforehand, we knew she had felt unsettled, but it still came as a shock. Looking back, I wondered if I had gone too far in my desire to look after my little nest and keep everyone close and safe. Maybe our conservative ideas felt stifling or even suffocating to our daughter. In any case, she was curious about the world beyond our family and friends, and when other friendship groups welcomed her into their more expansive lives, she was ready to spread her wings with them. It felt as if the more we tried to hold our firstborn close and keep her safe, the more her inner wrestling grew. It all came to a head one night when, while the rest of the family slept, she slipped away and disappeared.

Discovering her absence the next morning, I felt like an absolute failure. Everything around me seemed to spin, and my stomach felt like it was full of rocks. The world had tipped upside down. Most of all, I was frightened for her. *Where was she? Was she safe? Who was she with, and could they be trusted?* I blamed myself for not knowing how to 'get it right' and being powerless to help her. I realised that so much of my parenting had been driven by my desire to rewrite my story. I had struggled so much with knowing that I was truly loved, so I was desperate for my children to know how cherished and accepted they were. More than anything, I wanted to give them a good, safe start to life—with no doubts attached. Protecting our children had been my intention, but the harder I had tried, the more frustrated my daughter had become. For much of my life, I had battled my insecurities; now it seemed my worst fears were coming true.

When I realised our daughter had left, my earlier lofty vow of wanting our children to know they were loved and secure disintegrated before my eyes and felt suddenly hollow. My confidence was in pieces, yet I still had four more children who needed love and parenting. At that moment, I wished each one had arrived with a personal instruction manual filled with perfect solutions.

Christmas was approaching, but instead of anticipating a joy-filled time of celebration, I felt as if I was heading into open-heart surgery. I needed to find my courage and trust that things would work out eventually, but for a while, my faith was severely challenged. Our daughter did indeed come back to us, but it was a gradual process. We all changed a little, and a lot, broadening our views and stretching our hearts. We eventually learned to let go, knowing that, despite our flaws, we'd done our best and hoped that our parenting had been 'good enough'.

God had always been my anchor, but as I learned to stop 'white knuckling' my way through life and began letting go of what I'd been holding onto so tightly, I felt myself beginning to breathe a little easier. My need for control was replaced with a longing to experience more of God and His love and freedom, and increasingly my heart stretched open, letting Him into every part of my life completely. Even when I had nothing left to give, I discovered He was always enough.

7

Pathways of Grief

IT WASN'T UNTIL OUR three sons ended up in a motorbike accident that I discovered there was another dimension to my faith. Suddenly, I became acutely aware that 'guardian angel' was not just a comforting little phrase that people throw around but that angels are real and more involved in our lives than I'd ever realised.

That day, our eldest son, who escaped unhurt, came running in from the paddocks. "Mum! Dad!" he cried, his face white as a sheet, "There's been a terrible accident." He was carrying his youngest brother in his arms, and with one look, we knew we had no time to lose and made our way to the nearest hospital.

For the next forty-eight hours, we sat by our little boy's bedside, sending up prayers and willing him to be alright. Finally, he was taken from the intensive care unit into surgery. Watching him being wheeled away was a harrowing experience for us all. Once again, I was gripped with fear. Once again, I hadn't been able to keep my children safe.

Thankfully, a few days later, our precious five-year-old was happily back at home, sitting up at our kitchen bench colouring-in, when he looked up casually and said, "You know that time when I was in hospital . . ." We all froze and listened intently. He was a boy of few words, and we had been hoping he would soon be able to verbally process what had happened. Sure enough, he went on, "When I was having my operation, an angel came. He was big and handsome, with golden hair and a sword, and he was as tall as the stairs! He put his hand on my shoulder and told me, 'It's going to be alright!' and after that, I didn't feel scared." Then, just as simply as he had started talking about it, he turned around and went back to his colouring, as if it was the most natural and normal story in the world.

The rest of us looked at each other in surprise. This was the first time we had heard our son mention angels, but clearly, he was sure of what he was saying. It opened up a whole new level of appreciation for the spiritual realm. I had always presumed Phil and I were responsible for keeping our family safe. Now we realised we were not on our own after all. Our family was surrounded by angels who guarded us and watched out for us, even when we were unaware of them. It made me wonder if I, too, had a guardian angel looking out for me from my earliest days.

OVER THE NEXT FEW years, we were stretched in several directions, and we needed all the help our guardian angels had to offer. Both of my parents were now in their eighties, and as their health deteriorated, we needed to be more involved in their care. Once, in a surge of slight panic, I found myself whispering a half-prayer, "God, I don't know if I can do this." Quick as a flash, I remembered Mum telling me that those had been her very words when they had first considered adopting me. Now I took strength from that prayer. My mum *had* done it. She had given me a home even when she felt she couldn't, and now this was my opportunity to give back.

My parents soon settled into a nearby aged-care residence, although my mum spent a lot of her time in hospital. My thoughts turned to how our relationship had started with loss—Mum and Dad couldn't have biological children, which carried its own sorrow, and I, as a relinquished baby, was separated from my first mother. Yet here we were, decades later, our lives freshly interwoven. In recent years, my parents had lived a more harmonious life as they found more freedom and understanding in their faith and with each other. Now, with Mum away in the hospital frequently, Dad's favourite pastime was to watch nature programmes on television in his comfy chair. One evening, not long after I returned home from visiting him, I received a phone call from the nurse who had been looking after him. "I'm sorry," she told me matter-of-factly, "but your father has passed away." I was so shocked that I said to her, "I'm sorry, but you've rung the wrong person. I was with him only a few hours ago." I felt sorry for her that she had made such a mistake. But she repeated her words. *How could this be true?* Feeling unheard and misunderstood, I decided I needed to put Phil on the phone to explain the situation to her. Only then did it dawn on me that Dad had passed away. I was in disbelief. He had never been one to give hundreds of hugs or easily express how he felt, but he had always wanted the best for me. In his later years, he had shown remorse about some of his behaviour in the past, and he had always been a loving grandfather to my children. Ultimately, he was my dad, and he had given me the gift of a home and a family.

Tears came easily then. Phil and I went to see him immediately, pausing when we arrived as I felt a surge of sickness rise. My sister joined us there, and we said our goodbyes. My dad was now finally free from years of enduring pain. He had passed away in his comfy chair watching his favourite nature programme, and I thought that was a very kind way for him to go.

After Dad passed away, my visits to Mum increased. It was upsetting to see her worsen quickly to the point where she needed constant medical care. And then, unbelievably, just three weeks later, Phil's father sadly passed away too. He left behind a legacy of faith, strength of character, and integrity. Our hearts were torn, our grief and emotions raw, but there was even more loss to follow.

As Mum became weaker and bedridden, she was eager for the time to arrive when she too would be called to heaven. She knew it was coming very soon. When my sister phoned in the middle of the night, Phil and I went to be with Mum, hoping to be of comfort in her last moments. As she laboured to breathe, her nurse explained that she was likely finding it hard to let go. Hearing this, we reassured Mum that it was alright to leave when she felt ready to go. As her breaths became more faint and irregular, and knowing it would be a solace to her, I asked everyone if we could pray. Leaning closer to Mum, I whispered a gentle prayer ending with, "God please receive our mum into Your arms and let her be with You." With that, a tangible peace covered the room like a blanket, and Mum took her last breath. She was finally in heaven, the place she'd been longing for.

Desiring to honour Mum and Dad, I read some of their favourite verses at Mum's funeral. As I walked onto the stage, I was shaking and wondered how I would find my voice. Glancing at the stairs to the left of me, the thought came that I could simply run down them and out of the room if I had to. Thankfully, the pastor's hand gently touched my back in support at that moment. It was such a small act but enough to instil courage, and my words flowed freely as I shared a portion of Psalm 91:1 "Those who live in the shelter of the Most High will find rest in the shadow of the Almighty . . ." (NLT). My parents had requested it on repeat during the previous year; now it was a farewell echo.

Within seven weeks, the two people who had welcomed me into their ready-made family had passed away. Our connection may not have been biological, but for as long as I can remember, they had been my parents.

The following spring, we grieved another loss as Phil's mum—a woman I looked up to, who had loved and accepted me like a daughter—also passed away. Losing all four of our parents within ten months brought a torrent of emotions and plunged me into a deep season of grief.

Grief is such a small word to contain such a big range of feelings. As I considered each parent's story, I realised the impact of this cumulative loss on my life and faith had been huge. During the time leading up to their passing, there was a gradual awareness of what was to come. This anticipated grief paved the way ahead, allowing portions of sadness to rise up as we journeyed through it. Watching their wellness diminish brought heartache, but I also experienced a sense of peace and felt carried during these times. That is not to say I calmly went through these months without tears or setbacks, but rather opening myself up to the reality of pain and loss created a way for me to heal over time, allowing a deep sense of comfort. I had longed for them to be treated with dignity and kindness throughout their winter season and tried my best to help this be so.

Sometimes, friends asked me if I truly felt grief, wondering whether my adoption gave me a degree of separation from these feelings. I cannot speak for every adoptee since everyone has their own experience, but questions like this reminded me of when people would say, "They are not your *real* parents . . ." and I would not know how to respond. Naturally, there was a duality of sorts, as I wondered whether my feelings would have been the same if I had stayed with my biological parents and they had passed away. However, that was not my story, and it did not make my grief for my adoptive parents any less genuine. Like my acceptance for being both Lynne *and* Sheri, it was not an either/or question but a both/and, as I acknowledged my family tree includes two sets of parents— one biological and one adopted. I am unsure whether those of us who have been adopted tend to process grief differently, but I know that a great many carry the shadow of loss with them through their lifetime.

❧♡❧

As I PROCESSED MY grief along with managing the realities of family life and work, my health took a hit. In a season where my energy was depleted, I felt like I was drowning in a sea of overwhelm. I needed to sleep and rest most of the time, and everything came to a grinding halt. Although I was accustomed to being productive and active, I now needed to learn how to simplify my life.

Supportive friends patiently came alongside me and genuinely cared for me. We celebrated my fortieth birthday by sharing a meal on a long banquet table with fairy lights and music. Birthdays have been bittersweet over the years, but these friends felt like ministering angels refilling my heart, and I cherished every moment of our time together.

Aware of my search for healing and wholeness during this time, encouraging friends also invited me to a church conference a few hours away. As soon as we arrived my heart opened. The atmosphere, music and message were life-giving to me, and for the first time, I experienced a side of my faith that I had previously only imagined—one that was colourful, loving and free. When prayer was offered, I quickly accepted. I wept as a wave of love and compassion surged over me, trickling into all the cracks and crevices of my heart where I'd previously been hurting. God's love had always been a reliable anchor, but when I was prayed for, I felt His deep love for me in a brand-new way. He brought beauty from the ashes of my life, and it was the most beautiful exchange. Over the years I can see how He has safely led me through my journey—a lifelong journey of discovery which continues to unfold.

I earnestly began looking for ways to see beauty in each day, even in the small, seemingly insignificant things. I read the book *One Thousand Gifts* by Ann Voskamp about intentionally looking for specific things to be thankful for in the midst of life's difficulties, and it helped me readjust my focus. Random things would often capture my attention like a ladybird on a leaf, a bird singing, the depth of colour in the surrounding farmland, or the way cool water feels when swimming on a hot summer's day. In this way I would intentionally look up, keeping my senses tuned to the beauty evident in everyday life.

Counselling became an essential part of my healing as I unloaded my stories and understood the need to dial back my expectations of what I could manage. I needed to replace long-held beliefs and address the grief that had compounded over the years from my earliest beginnings. Feelings and thoughts I had pushed down long ago now bubbled to the surface, and instead of glossing over past difficulties, I needed to start telling myself the truth. For the most part, this was intensely challenging, but it also opened the door to new realisations about my history. Rather than ignore or make light of it, I began to see my life through the lens of having been adopted. For the first time, I stopped saying, "Everything's fine" when I wasn't feeling fine. One counsellor, after hearing my life story, gave me profoundly helpful advice which enabled me to mark a line in the sand. "From this day onwards," they said, "all self-blame and self-hatred need to go. You need to commit to re-parenting yourself and writing your own story going forward." Once I started this journey, I felt less invisible in the world. Owning my adoption story and accepting that no aspect of my life was unaffected by it was unexpectedly freeing, renewing my sense of purpose and belonging in the world.

My newfound freedom highlighted something I'd always known in a primal way but could never quite put my finger on. There was so much secrecy surrounding the topic of adoption, and despite its potential positives, there was an element of distress in navigating the entire process. The common narrative at the time was to 'never speak of it again', and so many important stories and memories were subsequently locked away and forgotten by those involved.

This struck me particularly one day when a lady, who had known Mum nearly forty years earlier, came up to me at church. "I remember meeting your mum years ago when I was a teenager," she said. "She was holding this little baby girl in her arms, and that baby was you, and she said, 'Look what I've been given.'" Now, decades later, she shared the scene with me as a grown woman and was able to offer me another small piece of the puzzle of my beginnings. I wondered why she had never mentioned it before. It was as if women of her generation were hesitant to divulge anything to do with adoption, for fear they might be sharing a secret that ought to stay hidden. Over time, the threads of my story were slowly being sewn together, but I couldn't help questioning if the tapestry would ever be fully complete.

8

Secrets

A FEW YEARS HAD PASSED since Phil and I had lost our parents, and I was wondering again about pursuing what felt like a risky endeavour—finding out more about my paternal side. I had always taken my mother's words that my biological father wasn't interested, as 'fact'. But there was another side to the story.

Our children can indeed teach us so much—and even more so, perhaps, as they grow older. My eldest daughter, who was in her mid-twenties by this point, was doing the dishes with me one day when the topic of searching for my birth parents came up. After a thoughtful pause, my daughter gently said something along the lines of, "Mum . . . I try, but I really struggle to understand why it feels so important for you to know about your biological family. I've always had parents who loved me. It's just so different."

Those tender words settled into my mind and heart and brought with them a sense of clarity. Hearing the respect and understanding in my daughter's response, and her desire to grasp how I might be feeling, stitched up part of my heart-wound in a beautifully healing way. Her words also brought a sweeping sense of relief. I realised that what my daughter was saying was that, despite all we had been through together, she had always felt loved.

Along with her insights came a small pinch of pain as I realised how hard it is for people to understand how it feels if they have not experienced adoption. It was as though a lightbulb went on in my mind, igniting a spark of an idea to help bring understanding where possible about this often-delicate subject.

It struck me as ironic that we often understand animals better than we do humans. I think of the lambs that have been separated from their mothers, crying out in our neighbour's paddock. Hearing them baa-ing, it seems to me they just desperately want their mama ewes. It was similar to when we were dairy farming. Whenever the young calves were separated from the cows, there was such a din. Both cow and calf let everyone know they'd prefer to be together by making plenty of noise about it. Interestingly, even though farmers have to carry on with the process regardless, they naturally understand and expect this trauma response. But while the pain of separation is acknowledged in animals, this hasn't always been the case with human babies and their mothers.

Back when closed adoptions were the norm, it was thought that a baby only needed to be nurtured and cared for—who provided that care wasn't deemed to be as important. Now, however, we know differently. A few years ago, I read a story about a baby whose mother asked some bystanders at a supermarket checkout to watch her baby in her pram for a moment while she went back to the aisle to get something. The baby was in the care of kind, capable people, yet she began crying as soon as she and her mother were separated. The baby instinctively knew and felt comforted when her mother was close and felt anxious when she was not.

My heart raced when I read that story. Something about the article made me feel so uncomfortable that I couldn't finish reading it. It was as if I was subconsciously agreeing with that little baby's cry. I had spent so many years trying to be 'normal' and accepting of my adoption. Yet now, at the age of fifty, as I emerged from a season of physical and mental exhaustion, I finally understood that this early separation experienced by adopted babies leaves an imprint of hurt and abandonment. There's no doubt that genuine hugs, love and affection between adopted children and their families go a long way towards creating a sense of wholeness and inner peace. But because of the lack of bonding and attachment with the birth mother, there can be a fragmented sense of belonging and connection, and for many people, this sense of internal disruption is sadly never resolved.

The reality is that the early thinking that an infant arrives with no attachment sets up all parties for misunderstanding. Throughout the years, comments like, "Just be thankful you're still here" or, "Just be grateful you have a family," do not acknowledge the fundamental longing we have to be connected on some level to our biological roots. The Welsh word *hiraeth* captures this beautifully, describing a deep sense of longing or yearning for a part of our past, like a grief that prevails, lingering just below the surface. No wonder so many adoptive families wrestle with a sense of disconnect. The grief is often silent and unexpressed, tucked away somewhere deep.

When we're ready, that grief can lead us to search for answers that help us make sense of our stories and this can result in the opportunity to either offer or receive forgiveness. My curiosity to understand and learn more motivated me to start another journey studying for a Diploma in Family Support. Part of the course included papers in counselling and social work, and as my assignments asked for research about family systems, I was drawn to articles on adoption and attachment. Tutors were encouraging, and open dialogue was robust and thought-provoking, leading me to a greater understanding of myself and others.

It didn't take long before I came across an old newspaper article that brought greater clarity to the narrative of that era. It went into detail about a hostel caring for single mothers and their babies and included a photo showing babies lined up on the floor together. At the time, these hostels may have offered a safe alternative for unmarried mothers, but something in my heart lurched as I looked at those beautiful babies about to go to new homes. I thought of the painful experiences of their mothers as well, each with very difficult decisions to make. Now, as I embraced research concerning the separation between mother and baby and the potential impact of this initial disruption on future healthy attachment, I sensed a shift in my desire to search again, this time on my paternal side. A new chapter of my story was about to begin.

IT FELT LIKE VENTURING into unknown territory once again, but eventually, I leaned into my desire to search for my biological father. I decided it was time to do whatever I could, just in case he was out there somewhere. My courage was sparked when a friend assured me, "It's never too late!"—but still, I hesitated. *What if he didn't want his long-lost daughter turning up out of the blue? And could I handle the rejection if he didn't want anything to do with me?*

In my hesitancy, I talked over my circumstances with a tutor from my course who had a similar story to mine, She understood the secrecy and shame aspects of the past but was compassionate, and urged me to go ahead. "It is natural and normal to want to know the roots of your family tree," she reminded me.

The next person I spoke to about my intentions was my birth mother. It felt important to check in with her—not to seek her permission, but to explain the curiosity I felt about my heritage on my paternal side. Deep down, I also wanted her approval. Our contact over the years had dwindled and was not very regular by this point. It struck me that there are so many secrets kept in the dark which need to be brought into the light so people can heal. Still, I wanted to respect her feelings.

Sandra and her husband were not surprised when I told them of my intentions. They reassured us that their three adopted children had all searched and reunited with their biological families, and encouraged us to go ahead. More importantly, she provided us with his middle name to make the search easier. This was a pivotal moment for me. I was aware Sandra still carried so much hurt from that time in her life, and although she was willing to help, I was struck by her sadness.

Over the years I had tried, with limited success, to reassure her that she hadn't done the wrong thing, and to help her feel better about it all. But rather than bringing her to a place of peace, it had only nurtured my misplaced guilt and sense of responsibility for circumstances that, as a tiny baby, were out of my control. Sadly, as time went on, talking about the past became more upsetting to Sandra, and I often ended up being misunderstood. Eventually, although I felt grief over it, I had to make peace with the fact that it wasn't my fault, and I couldn't carry her pain. Ironically, truthful insights can often land when someone unexpectedly speaks them into your life. When receiving feedback from an assignment which included parts of my own story, my tutor commented, "You do know this wasn't your fault, don't you?" For some reason, on that day, those words finally stuck, and another healing layer folded over my heart.

Motivated by these freeing thoughts, I felt released to start moving forwards, and the quest began. Mindful about embracing our present family and circumstances, we connected often, even though there was always plenty going on for everyone, and this brought a much-needed sense of togetherness. We used to watch a show called *This Is Us* on television. As the series progressed, the adopted child in the story often found it hard to fit in and ultimately went on a quest to find his birth father. The search and reunion storyline inspired me. I also watched another series which showcased families who had become estranged or separated over time. Many of them involved adoptions, researching the family's history and ultimately locating and reuniting people with their biological parents or family members. Interestingly, the show highlighted the number of people who were looking for family members and the difficulties they continued to face without help. Adoption law was still stuck in the 1950s, and files on any 'closed adoptions' were unable to be opened. *How could it be that so many people could enjoy the hobby of finding ancestors online, yet when people were looking for family members through the lens of adoption, there was so much resistance to finding answers?*

When I had tried to search online on previous occasions, my success had been limited. It had been at least thirty years since I met my birth mother and she had told me about seeing my birth father's company car. That company had since gone out of business, and whenever I searched for my father's name online, several people came up but no real lead. Now, however, I had something more specific to work with. My birth father's middle name was a crucial piece of the puzzle, so I resumed my online search to see if any trails might lead me back to him.

Accepting that my birth father might have already passed away, we checked the births, deaths and marriages register, but found nothing. Next, we searched the electoral role—and found his name and his general location! Motivated by this, I began scouring social media, much like a detective searching for clues. I clicked on one profile after another, and finally, one turned up who appeared to be his brother!

Looking through the friend list of this man who I hoped might be my uncle, we found a profile that could have been my father. We decided that just in case we were wrong, we would reach out to this man first. He was a retired vicar of St. Paul's Church in Auckland. This gave me hope. If anyone was going to understand our search, a vicar surely would.

Rather than contact him online, Phil and I decided to look the vicar up and pay him a visit. We drove two hours before arriving at the retirement home where he now resided, and, taking hold of a handful of courage and hope, we asked at the reception desk if we could see the man whom I hoped would turn out to be my uncle. The receptionist kindly replied that he was out that afternoon, but if we left our phone number, she would let him know we had visited and ask him to contact us.

We sat in the foyer for a while, feeling rather amazed to have come this far. While we waited we considered what to do next. I felt a flurry of excitement and anticipation, thinking how close I might be to connecting the last piece of my heritage. My imagination took flight. *My uncle walks around these buildings. This is his home, his community—he knows these people.* It felt grounding somehow. We eventually headed out to the gardens and took a short walk around before heading back to the car.

We didn't have to wait long before we heard back from him. Just two hours later, while we were still driving home, the phone rang. My husband and I looked at each other. *Could this be the phone call?* We both knew it in our hearts. As Phil pulled the car over to the side of the road, we heard a kindly voice on the other end. "Hello, I believe you were looking for me today?"

My eyes welled up. After so much wondering, we had finally made a connection. Thankfully, Phil enthusiastically answered, "Hello, thank you for ringing us back so soon. This might seem a little unusual but we're looking for someone who gave a baby up for adoption fifty years ago and wondered if he might be your brother?" Placing the speakerphone on, Phil and I took turns explaining the situation slowly and carefully. If these men *were* related, we wanted to get a sense of how close they were to avoid creating any problems. So much information had been kept secret and reunions were so rare that we had no idea how our query might be received. *If his brother was my biological father, would the news come as a shock? Were we revealing a secret he may have tried to keep for decades? Would it upset another whole family?* In the end, we simply explained that we would appreciate any information that would help us find my father or his family.

Have you experienced the feeling of being both comforted and strengthened at the same time? I hope you have. There was no shame, criticism, avoidance or judgement in his strong, gentle voice, only love and acceptance—like an extension of God's love coming right down the phone line into our conversation.

In the past, I had grown used to hearing words of rejection or belittlement. These were mostly unintentional, I hope, because of the stigma of shame surrounding unmarried mothers and society's reluctance to update the outdated language and beliefs around these 'unwanted babies'. My cheeks would glow bright red with embarrassment as I endured another uncomfortable reaction, and this was reinforced when I sent away for my original birth certificate several years earlier. Up to this point, I had only ever seen my adoptive birth certificate with my changed name and new parents listed. When the document arrived, I saw my original name, Sheri, next to my birth mother's name, but there was no name listed at all for my father. Instead, the ugly word 'illegitimate' was written on an accompanying piece of paper, for anyone to read. It's a word that has always stung.

But there was no ugliness in my newly discovered uncle's words. His deep voice, reverberating through the phone line, spoke only kindness. "Yes, that sounds like my brother John," he said. "It all makes sense." He was careful with his words and eventually suggested, "Why don't I just give you his phone number so you can contact him directly." He explained that his brother had been 'through the mill' over the past few years, and gently prepared us to tread carefully. This was a surprise! We had hoped he might act as our 'middle person' so that contacting my father wouldn't be too much of a shock for him. But it appeared he was saying, "Go for it!" He assured us that he had seen enough of these stories and situations over the years to know that only good would come of it.

Knowing how much it had come to mean to me, and also because I was half-frozen about what to do next, Phil picked up the phone that very night and dialled the number given to us. "Hello, is that John?" he asked. "You don't know me, but I think I might be married to your daughter." He then went on to ask if he had fathered a baby girl fifty years ago who had been adopted out. There was a silence, momentarily followed by a "Yes," and, "Oh my goodness." Naturally, he was very surprised! They politely talked, gathering details to make sure he was indeed the person we were looking for, while I paced in and out of the room wondering what to do or say next. It was a brief discussion—he said he was tired after finishing work, but he conveyed something along the lines of the way forward being positive. Not wanting to delay, we asked if we could perhaps meet him when we would be in Auckland again, a few days later. He replied that he was going away with his family for the weekend but would be back Sunday afternoon if that might suit.

If that might suit?!

After years of wondering and not knowing, meeting my biological father was now looking like a real possibility! I didn't quite know whether to feel excited or nervous or scared, and truthfully, I felt a mix of all three. We keenly felt the importance of what was unfolding, and with a strong sense of expectation, I looked forward to putting more of the puzzle pieces of my family tree back together.

9

Great Expectations

A DAY BEFORE WE set out to make the journey to meet my biological father, I was in the kitchen, chatting to our family about our recent phone call. When I said, somewhat casually, that we were going up to meet him, nobody could believe it. There was a long pause, after which my eldest son put words to everyone's feelings, "Wait, is this really happening?" I recalled his sage advice on previous occasions, "It might not be easy, but it will be worth it," and I was reminded again of the decades-long journey it had taken to get to this point in my story. That moment brought some reverence and weight to the uniqueness of the situation—this was not just your usual weekend activity but a potentially life-altering moment in our family's history. And it *was* happening.

I'd thought carefully about the implications of meeting my biological father and decided that we wouldn't put any expectations on our children to meet him or form a relationship with him at this stage. After all, they'd already had two sets of grandparents in their lives. On top of that, there were so many unknowns. After watching their relationship with my birth mother dwindle over the years, and taking into consideration they were adults now, it didn't feel as important for them to meet him right away. I wanted it to ultimately be their choice, if and when the time was right. Maybe later in life they would want to know more about their roots, but for now, it was enough for Phil and I to meet John in person, and then we'd take it from there.

Phil was assured and calm as we set off on our adventure, and I was thankful for his solid strength. As we approached Auckland, the familiar feelings of self-doubt crept in. This was a day I had pondered about on and off for years, and countless questions were spinning through my mind about meeting a parent at the age of fifty. *How would it go? Would he accept me or shut me out?* My uncle had indicated that his brother now had a family of his own, including children who would have been slightly younger than me. *Would I get to meet them someday?*

We had arranged to meet at John's house at 3 p.m., and then we would go for coffee somewhere. We found a parking spot on a nearby street, but at the last minute, I froze. I couldn't believe it. I was about to meet my biological father, and it was as if I had a terrible case of stage fright. *What if all of this was a huge mistake? What if he wasn't interested in me at all? What if he didn't like me?* It was my newly found uncle's reassuring words, "Only good will come of it" that gave me enough momentum to press forward. I knew my worth wasn't tied up in this meeting, but in that moment, any sort of logic seemed to fly away. I experienced flight, fright and fawn reactions in quick succession, before finally settling on freeze. Turning to Phil, I asked, "Please can you go first? Maybe just say a quick hello to check this is going to be alright." He half laughed, understanding the push-pull feelings of the day, and off he went to do just that. In a matter of minutes, he was walking back to me with a smile and a thumbs-up signal. "It's all okay," he reassured me. "Come and meet him."

Walking up John's driveway, tentatively smiling, my heart was nearly pounding out of my chest. *Could everyone else hear it, too?* Then, there he was. A normal human being, linked to me by biology. Meeting me at the door in a checked shirt, jeans, and bare feet, he extended an arm and touched my elbow before giving me a quick kiss on the cheek. It was a surreal moment. A meeting between a father and daughter after fifty years required courage—courage on both sides, I would guess.

John welcomed us in and offered a cup of tea, and instead of going out, we all sat down together. We tried to chat about life in the best way we could, recognising the huge distance of time that had passed and all the life experiences that had been lived within it. *How do you fill in the blanks of fifty years in a few moments?* Sitting there on his couch, I felt like a six-year-old girl again, my eyes taking in every detail of this person who, until this morning, I would not have known if I had passed him in the street. We stayed for a couple of hours. He was cautious but friendly. John was retired and now lived by himself, but he showed us some photos of his family. It was a very surreal time; there was such a mix of emotions as I tried to reconcile the fact that all these people were related to me. I showed him several photos of our family and one of me as a girl. Between us, we were trying to fill in the gaps that had been created by so many years apart. Mysteries were finally being solved as I uncovered the remaining missing links of my family tree.

John was almost apologetic as he explained his ups and downs over the years, voicing concerns, and perhaps even some regrets, about my adoption. He confessed that all those years ago he hadn't known what to do. "Times have changed," he said. "Adoption was so common back then. Fifty years ago, even if fathers wanted to see their partner and baby, they were generally sent away and told to get on with their lives, well away from the mother." He noticed me looking at the bright orange cushions on the couch where we sat and commented that he had bought them for this special occasion. I'm not sure if it was a joke, but somehow the light-heartedness of his words felt validating.

Knowing how common adoptions were around the time I was born, I understood what John was trying to say. I wasn't looking to blame anyone, I just longed for answers, and he was able to fill in some of the blanks. As we prepared to leave, I asked if he would be willing for Phil to take a photo of the two of us together. "Yes, of course," he said, "that would be a compliment!" As we stood together for the photo, I realised that although it hadn't been the easiest day, something inside me had shifted. As a child, I often wondered why I felt so out of place, so different to those around me. Standing beside my biological father, it was as if another missing piece had finally fallen into place.

As we were leaving, Phil had the presence of mind to mention we would love to meet the rest of his family, including my siblings. Finding my half-brothers and sisters had been a great motivation in seeking out my father. I was a little surprised, then, when he responded cautiously. "Well, this is only day one. Let's see what happens." Any illusions I might have had about meeting my siblings on the first day had already faded. But as we farewelled each other, John said he would be in touch, and I realised I simply had to be patient. Nevertheless, as we walked to the car, I felt as if I was walking on air.

It turned out that the weekend brought more than one reunion. In the early hours of the following morning, our eldest daughter arrived home after living in London for a few years. It was priceless to be able to hug her at the airport and share the story of meeting my biological father. As I explained the details to her, we were all able to process it together amidst the catching up.

I HAD OFTEN WISHED for a reunion with my biological father's side of the family, and was thankful that I had been given the chance to meet him. I remember someone saying to me, however, "Be careful what you wish for." Truthfully, I didn't realise the journey ahead would be so challenging to navigate, and without a doubt, it was only my faith and family that gave me the strength to persevere through it. Although I was happy with the outcome of finally meeting my birth father, there were parts of it that were upsetting. I very quickly realised that while he was polite enough to meet me, he also wanted to keep me at arm's length. Any dreams I'd had of being welcomed into the wider family were met with disappointment. John had already explained that he was a private person, so we understood that we needed to give him time and space to get used to the idea of having me in his life. I realised that I had been pondering how to show up in his life for some time, whereas he had received a phone call out of the blue from a daughter he'd never met.

Although he had been willing to meet me, it was clear that he was not comfortable letting his children know about their half-sister. I hoped that with time there would be acceptance, but at this stage, it was bittersweet, as if I was a birth announcement waiting to happen—and way too late. Phil reassured me by saying this would be a marathon, not a sprint, but even so, I felt disheartened. *Perhaps my expectation that I would one day meet my family members was simply too high.*

I was thankful we had at least managed a reunion, but it still felt partial. When we were going through the photo albums together, John had pointed out three other children—my half-brothers and sister. One had sadly passed away from cancer at the age of twenty-five, and I could tell by the tone of his voice that John was still keenly affected by his death. I was sad too that I would never get to know my younger half-brother. Even so, I held onto the hope that, in time, I would get to meet my other siblings whom I might share similarities with. This shared connection and close resemblance is what I have loved seeing develop in the family my husband and I have created together—the same eyebrow lift or laugh, similar character traits or abilities or ways of caring. We have a treasure trove of shared experiences, and they are each part of a beautiful, messy picture that I love with all my heart. I was mindful to keep my main focus on my 'now' family which was loving and fulfilling in itself. But there was still an undercurrent of hopefulness that I would one day make more connections with my extended birth family.

I kept in touch with John occasionally by text, and over the next few years, we met a couple of times for coffee. Each time, I enquired if he felt any closer to allowing me to meet his family. His concern was fuelled by worry about their reaction, and I lacked the confidence and forth-rightness to make introductions myself without his permission. One Father's Day, a text arrived from my biological father simply saying he was thinking of me. It was brief, but it brought a tear to my eye. Meanwhile, I was figuring out how it looked to respect his point of view, since Phil and I had agreed from the outset we wouldn't risk upsetting anyone. All these years later, there were still secrets, and it felt very uncomfortable that I was being kept hidden from my extended family when it was surely just normal human curiosity to want to meet them.

In every story there are treasures hidden away, waiting to be found. One of these was the opportunity to develop a relationship with my biological uncle—the vicar I had spoken with on the phone. Since he had been accepting and welcoming—so much so, that it felt as if the Lord Himself was somewhere nearby—I searched for him online and found some of his sermons. They were soothing to listen to, and as he enthusiastically unpacked faith and God's love, I was glad I had heard them.

He had said at the time that he would keep us in his prayers and hoped to meet us face-to-face someday, so on one trip to Auckland to see my birth father, I poured out my heart to God and asked for the chance to meet my uncle also. Well, a cannon must have gone off in heaven because, on our way there, we received a message from John asking if it would be alright if his brother—my uncle—joined us for coffee! Filled with anticipation, I walked into the café and finally met the vicar who had initially brought us together. I can barely explain how it felt to see both my biological father and my uncle together, greeting us warmly!

There was a light and warmth about my uncle, and when he extended his arms for a hug, there was a feeling of acceptance and connection that was undeniable. He didn't shy away from the hard questions, but he was thoughtful and kind as he leaned in to ask me to share what it was like for me to be adopted. He also said he recognised their mother's eyes in mine which held meaning for me having long wondered about family resemblances. His laugh was jolly and fun and contagious, and having him there made my biological father feel so much more comfortable. He also said he and my biological father should both come down for a road trip as he had very close friends who lived near us, and then they could hopefully meet our family too. It seemed full of promise, and as we left that day, my wounded heart felt covered by yet another layer of healing and warmth.

Being from New Zealand, I had thought about the Māori emphasis on knowing our heritage and understanding our roots, our *whakapapa*. As part of my course in counselling, each of us had been asked to share our *whakapapa*—giving respect and honour to where we came from and who our family were. I had to explain to the tutor I knew nothing of my biological roots and wondered how I should progress with that part of the assessment. It was like being back at school, once again not knowing how to describe my family tree.

I realised that if I was ever to find out more about my family, it would probably not come through John. As time passed, I sensed his uncertainty rise, and although he was polite, he remained guarded. I plucked up the courage to call him a couple of times, hoping he would eventually trust me enough to meet his family, but I just didn't feel like I could force my way in. Eventually, I realised John's permission was not a prerequisite to connecting with kin; it was my hesitancy holding me back. Increasingly,

I became aware of not colluding with his desire for secrecy, and I decided I needed to start being more proactive and assertive if I wanted to know more about my place in the world.

Family and friends suggested I look up my siblings' addresses without his knowledge, then simply turn up and introduce myself, but I was hesitant. My inner wrestling continued as I wondered what I should do next, but knowing I had the support of my uncle motivated me to not give up. He knew all along that it would be better for everyone if the past came out of hiding into the open.

I wish there had been more time to get to know my uncle before he passed away. Sadly, I missed his funeral as I only discovered his obituary while reading the paper. The news almost broke my heart. The first night after I found out, I was distraught. I woke up realising I was crying in my sleep, such was the profound loss I felt. Unfortunately, with his passing everything went even quieter, and I wondered if the candle of hope I had held onto had finally flickered out.

My uncle's empathetic, caring heart had been a gift to my own. He understood that everyone had their own story, and instead of correction and judgement, he offered me compassion and mercy. When he cheerfully said, "You can call me Uncle Bill," he had unwittingly (or maybe knowingly) grafted me into his family tree—a gesture that had made me feel valued and left a lasting imprint.

Now, not only had I lost my uncle, but I had to come to terms with the fact that I had been completely overlooked at his death, and my heart ached. It was a reality check, and at that point, any hope of being acknowledged on the paternal side of my family tree felt very far away indeed.

10

Weaving the Threads

LOOKING BACK, MY MISTAKE was perhaps waiting so long to be proactive in my search. Part of me had always trusted—or hoped—it would all turn out alright eventually; however, despite my best intentions, I had to accept I was making little progress with my birth father's family. I began to feel responsible for my biological father's uneasiness, and carried shame which was never mine to carry. A battle was raging within my mind and heart, and I was increasingly 'over' trying to convince my father that I was an 'okay' person who might one day meet the rest of my family.

It was a confusing and disappointing time, and it played tricks on my confidence. I thought about the scene in *Back to the Future* where the main character, Marty, was holding onto a photo of himself. Every time he looked at the photo, he realised he was gradually disappearing until he was nearly unable to function. I resonated with his identity crisis. As far as my paternal search went, I too felt unseen and unheard, bordering on invisible at times. Part of my identity was slowly fading, and if I left it too long, I worried that my roots might one day become untraceable.

Meanwhile, my own dear family became more and more concerned and wondered whether it was a good idea to maintain contact with my birth father without reciprocation. Dear friends talked it over with me as well, and together we prayed for reconciliation with my family members.

It was time to release John from any obligation to connect me with my extended family. One day, on one of our rare coffee meetups, I explained that we didn't want or need anything from him; I simply wanted to know about all the branches on my family tree. Phil tried to reassure him too, but John was unwavering. "I don't want to 'wreck' anything," he said.

I realised then that John was not being meanspirited or secretive—he was simply fearful of how finding out about me might impact his family relationships. "If you ever change your mind," I responded, seeing that nothing could persuade him, "you know where we are." As we said our farewells, Phil looked him in the eye and said, "You need to know that Lynne is the best thing that has ever happened to me." John nodded but was lost for words. I, on the other hand, was reminded at that moment what true love really is.

ABOUT A YEAR LATER, a good friend suggested that we pray together for healing. During this time, I had the beautiful impression of a very large extended family in a lush green field with mature trees behind them. People of every generation—grandparents, parents, children, and babies—were all enjoying their time together. In my heart, I was sure I was seeing the family Phil and I were creating together. I could see that our family would be loving, happy, blessed, and connected, with a strong and deep-rooted sense of belonging and encircled by God's love for us. It was such a vivid picture and helped me realise that despite any hurtful, confusing or disappointing events that had led to this point, it was important for me to focus on our family, both now and as we welcomed future generations. This came at an especially profound time as our first grandchild was due in a few months, also bringing the promise of hope for the future.

Another clear picture came during a time of prayer. This time I saw a scene from heaven. Jesus himself was holding our three babies lost to miscarriage, embracing them and looking at them with eyes filled with love. Looking at me with the kindest, most compassionate face I had ever seen, He said, "Aren't they beautiful?" I was so very comforted by this, and then, in amazement, I began noticing jewels everywhere and realised the whole place was sparkling. As I dived into a beautiful freshwater pool beneath a waterfall, I felt a sense of freedom and warmheartedness that I can barely express even now. I felt fresh, clean, whole, and loved, and that serene moment became a defining one in my life.

Around this time, when my eldest son asked me how the most recent visit with my father had gone, I was transparent about the fact that he was not keen on sharing his secret with his family. We talked honestly about the disappointment that what should have been such a natural relationship had been turned into something so secretive and shameful. "It looks like our family tree will have to start with me," I shared truthfully. As I said those words, my mind flashed back to the beautiful image I received during prayer of our big extended family enjoying a picnic together, offering hope and acceptance for the future.

SINCE I HAD BEEN unable to attend my uncle's funeral, a thought had struck me about visiting friends of his who lived nearby. I wondered if they might be open to meeting me, and by finding out more about him, I could perhaps build more of a picture of his life and eventually find some closure. During this time, I was realising how often I had placed other people's wishes ahead of my own in my search for answers. Trying to respect the feelings of others alongside my own was a tricky balancing act, but one I wanted to learn. So often, I would shelve the questions I sought answers to, concentrating instead on my own family, until that loud inner voice would say, "Keep going!" It was a turbulent time as I forced myself once again to silence my inner critic and face my fear of rejection, but my curiosity would not let it drop. Although I worried if it was appropriate to crash someone else's friendship like this, the overriding feeling was that this was something I needed to do. Too many times over the years, I had shrunk back when I could have pushed forward, and so, after a couple of attempts, I eventually sent them a message.

I was so relieved when I heard back from them, and they were happy to meet up for morning tea and a chat. Making the short drive just down the road, I arrived to a very warm welcome and wonderful conversations. They brought out some photos of times they had shared with my uncle, and we talked about my story—about which they were very understanding. They thought it was the most normal thing in the world to want to know more about a family connection, which immediately instilled in me a sense of warm reassurance. They shared more about my uncle's faith and mission trips along with more of his sermons. It was a remarkable meeting, and I wept with relief at being understood and validated.

Unexpectedly, they extended an invitation to my uncle's upcoming memorial service. Their acceptance was so refreshing, and initially, I was quite stunned. After staring at them with wide eyes, and double checking they thought it would be fine to attend, they responded, "Well he is your uncle after all, and you have every right to be there." Little did I know in that moment, what a sacred occasion it would be.

Meanwhile, during the lead-up to the memorial service, our first grandchild was born. What a joy it was to receive the call and hear the news, "We have a brand-new baby girl." Then came the celebrations, and the tears flowed. We were invited to come and meet this precious new family member, and we could barely keep away from the hospital. Each new baby is a miracle, and we were filled with wonder at this new life. We hugged, cried, and felt the holiness of that moment. Holding her in a tender embrace, we welcomed her into our family and prayed a blessing over her. We were simply elated.

The room went silent with anticipation as her name was announced. Our son and daughter-in-law had chosen a beautiful first name, linked to her side of the family, and Lynne for her middle name. I could scarcely believe it. Tears snaked down my cheek at this symbol of connection and belonging. After tussling with familial separation for decades, seeing my name passed down generationally was a humbling gift of love. It felt as though the cracks deep within me were being sealed and made whole, like the bowls mended with liquid gold in the ancient art of *Kintsugi*. The cuddles, songs and joy this little one brought to all of our lives was delightful. Legacy and lineage, linked with love.

✤♡✤

WHEN THE TIME CAME for my uncle's memorial service, a good friend sent me a message letting me know that an invitation had also been given on social media for people to attend. Initially, my family was slightly incredulous that I was seriously considering attending, but when they saw my intent, they were fully supportive.

We phoned my biological father, who had told me earlier that it would be a long way for us to come, and he did his best to dissuade us. We had already mentioned our desire to pay our respects without making a fuss or creating unwanted attention, and although he was standoffish, we replied, "Sorry, but we're coming." I wrestled again with feeling like an outsider, but then one of our daughters—the songbird of the family—gave me the words to the song "Way Maker," reminding me to believe and have courage. Bolstered by her faith and encouragement, I leaned into prayer and reminded myself of a verse which had become a favourite of mine: "For God has not given us a spirit of fear, but of power and of love, and of a sound mind" (2 Timothy 1:7).

A sense of determination and peace was rising. Although what I was about to do was out of character, it also truly felt like one of the most authentic things I could possibly do.

After a long journey to the far north, we arrived at a quaint, historic, beautiful old church. With my heart beating, I tried to stay discreetly 'in the background' to lessen my father's fears while also carrying a quiet certainty about being there. There was a peaceful presence, and we briefly met our new friends who warmly welcomed us. As we wandered around, admiring the beautifully crafted *korowai* that the Māori community he had served had draped over his grave as a symbol of honour, I could see my uncle was deeply loved and respected by the friends and family gathered there.

My heart skipped a few beats when I saw a woman alongside the chapel. I quickly turned and said to my husband, "I think that may be my sister!" We turned back to the group gathering and sat inconspicuously at the back, but the next minute, I felt a tap on my shoulder. It was a spine-tingling moment as I realised this was it! *What do I do now!?* I suddenly thought, *Am I about to be asked to leave?* Then, a cheerful voice said, "Are you Lynne?" With my heart beating a million beats to the second, I replied yes, and turned around with some trepidation. "Hi, I think I'm your sister," she said. "I only just found out!" It so happened that my father and my sister had travelled together, and only towards the end of their three-hour drive had he told her about the possibility of me being there—only ten minutes before they arrived! With those words, she leaned across, and we nearly fell into each other's arms. It was the most euphoric moment. I had never imagined it would feel so good to be welcomed into the warm, generous embrace of my sister!

I struggled to compose myself as we settled back to our respective places and the memorial service began. It seemed as if the ground had moved under my feet and shifted me onto solid ground. A sense of freedom rose in me that I hadn't experienced before. No longer was I holding onto someone else's secret. No longer was *I* a secret either! I wept as I listened to one person after another share a *karakia*, or prayer, along with their memories of my uncle. It was all so respectful and honouring. John seemed to accept that I was there, but at the same time, didn't know what to do with me. Even so, I felt very grateful to be present. After the service, my new sister and I spent a rather flurried time, sharing photos and trying to fill in some of the missing pieces in such a short amount of time—while also trying to ensure that our new relationship did not take precedence over the important proceedings of the day. My sister gave me the contact details of a few of the people who had been part of the day, and sometime later, I sent messages to several of them in an effort to be respectful and explain my appearance. Everyone was kind and accepting, appreciating the complexity of the circumstances. In fact, unbeknownst to me, my uncle had already told his family all about me!

As we drove away from the service, I felt somewhat overwhelmed, but in a good way. We decided to stay the night close by to give me the chance to pause and process everything that had unfolded. Finally, I had met a sister! She was seven years younger than me, super friendly, accepting and warm. All those years of wondering and waiting had finally resulted in a fruitful connection, and the sense of belonging was grounding and healing. I recognised that my prayers had been answered, and the ultimate "Where do I belong?" question was finally being revealed. I was finally emerging from the silence and shadows into the light.

A FEW DAYS LATER, I noticed a missed phone call from my father. I returned his call and was very surprised when he said, "I've had it all wrong. I've talked to all of the family, and everybody would like to meet you—the sooner the better!" *The sooner the better?* I could have fallen off my seat! Then he threw in another bombshell. "And guess what? You've got another sister who was also placed for adoption. She's really keen to meet you as well!"

I was so surprised by this turnaround. John passed on my aunty's phone number. When I called her later that week, we enjoyed a good conversation, asking and answering many questions about our family and heritage. He also passed on my adopted sister's phone number, but she had already been given mine and was so eager to make contact that she left me a message before I even finished talking to him! My sister was just as friendly and welcoming as anyone could wish for, and was excited to meet me. I was amazed to suddenly have a new aunt, a brother, *and* two new sisters! Everything was unravelling at speed, but in the best way—as though all the tangles and knots were being tidied up and the tapestry threads were beginning to form a complete picture at last.

Not long after this, we found ourselves heading to Auckland again, this time to meet the rest of the family: a half-brother, two half-sisters, cousins, partners, and an aunty who went to the effort to bring a lovely gift—a gloxinia plant with vibrant purple, velvet-like flowers—and a welcoming card signed by everyone there. I was so touched and grateful; everyone was very kind-hearted and inclusive and wanted to know what took me so long to meet them! We all sat at tables joined together at a nearby café and talked and laughed. We may not have *felt* exactly like family, but it didn't matter. It was more important to me that I had *found* my family. I didn't have to wonder and guess any more. I finally knew them and they knew me, and that was enough. On that day, something recalibrated inside me. It was a wonderful, precious time.

Someone had the presence of mind to take some photos of us, newly introduced to one another. I smiled to myself as I noticed behind us in the garden was a large *pikorua* (twist) representing love and connection, strength and unity between two people or between kin. Once, on a visit to New Zealand's South Island, Phil bought me a beautiful *pounamu* (greenstone) necklace in this very shape, and both of us were appreciative of its significance. I couldn't think of a more poignant backdrop to our family reunion.

MY AUNTY EXPLAINED THAT back in the era when I was born, their parents would have never accepted the idea of a baby born out of wedlock. Over the years I had learned that many women were sent away to other relatives to protect the family name and defuse a potential scandal. While adoption was thought to be a useful solution to the 'problem', thousands of families were subsequently fractured as a result of the shame and secrecy surrounding the process, and many adoptees and birth mothers still bear the wounds of the 'choices' that were forced upon them during those years. Even though many adoptions do have a safe and positive outcome, there is still much to be learned. One thing I wish people would understand is that even when an adoptee is happy and content in their adoptive family, it's normal for them to want to trace their biological family. When reunions are not possible due to archaic, closed adoption laws and long-held family secrets, this can create disruption, insecurity, and confusion for everyone involved. It's important, therefore, that we continue to talk about closed adoptions within our families and communities, removing the barriers of secrecy and enabling people to have the means and opportunity to know their kin and understand their place in their story.

As I took in the similarities and familiar mannerisms between my sisters and my daughters that day at the café, I felt filled with wonder at how my story had unfolded. My thankfulness for answered prayers spilt over, and I wanted to shout my gratefulness from the rooftops. I thought about how far I had come. I had started life as an 'illegitimate' baby girl in the eyes of the law, and for much of my life I had wrestled with my identity and feelings of inadequacy. Now I felt as if I had come home to myself. It had taken both tenacity and faith, and by pausing many times in the process and praying often I had been able to continue putting one step in front of the other. Thankfully, I had a very supportive, loving husband who had travelled this journey with me, and at times even carried me when it all felt too heavy. All the years of questioning, *Who am I? Where do I fit? Am I enough?* had finally melted into some form of understanding and acceptance. Somehow, on this day, I felt planted—I was healthy and alive, yes, but now I seemed to have a root system as big as the plant itself. There was a sense of completeness in finally meeting my family that day, and I will always be amazed that my dream was able to become a reality.

I was one of the fortunate ones, but I am aware that other people's experiences of adoption differ from my own. My heart goes out to all those who have journeyed through the complex feelings that accompany a search story or who are hitting roadblocks to finding out their history. My prayer is that everyone would experience a settled feeling of belonging, whether those long-hoped-for reunions ever happen or not. May any separations one day be mended and healed, and may each of us ultimately be established in a legacy of love.

Epilogue

SHORTLY AFTER WE MET, my two half-sisters and I arranged to have a weekend together. It would be a time to get to know each other more and catch up on our lives. When I arrived at the café we were meeting at for lunch, both of them came out to greet and welcome me, which really touched my heart. We stayed close to the beach and shared long conversations with tears and laughter. It was a treasured time.

The following day, we were walking along the beach in bursts of laughter, trying unsuccessfully to take a selfie in such a picturesque scene. When a friendly gentleman walked up to us and offered to take our photo for us, we were very appreciative and gladly accepted. We were so involved in our conversation that we initially didn't notice he was with a team that seemed to be working on some kind of assignment. Curious now, we inquired what it was about. It turned out he was a reporter, and during our conversation, he expressed an interest in our story of being reunited after a lifetime apart. He exchanged phone numbers with one of my sisters, and despite thinking how funny it was to bump into him that way, we assumed nothing would come of it. Surprisingly, he rang a few weeks later. He requested that he interview us all individually to put the pieces of our stories together, before publishing an article in the newspaper a few months later. We were a bit nervous, but we trusted our story to him and hoped it might encourage and inspire—and perhaps even help heal in some way—anyone who might read it.

Phil and I spent time with my birth mother beforehand to prepare her for the article, hoping to soften any hurt she might feel. This, sadly, was not an easy transition for her as some pain still lingered. When I explained to my brother and sister about the developing story, to my relief they were both pleased and supportive. Over the years, my sister and I have had countless conversations about all things adoption and cared for each other through our experiences. I will always be grateful to her for courageously leading the way as she searched for her birth mother.

My brother, who largely kept to himself and at one point exclaimed, "Well, I was your brother first!" also went on to search for his genealogy. Discovering his grandfather was of Māori heritage, he was welcomed onto their *marae*. This was a beautiful outcome, and he seemed finally at home and at peace within himself. My heart is relieved and comforted by this thought as sadly, a few months later, he lost his life while swimming in the ocean. The sea, which had been so healing and life-giving to my brother when he was five, ultimately stole his life decades later. Still, I was so glad that he had finally found his 'people' and discovered a state of belonging that is natural and normal for so many, but one that continues to be out of reach for others.

When the news article was published, I was pleasantly surprised by the readers who got in touch afterwards to share different aspects of their own adoption experiences. I felt humbled and thankful we were able to be part of a story that brought some hope to others, and it is my prayer that this book will do likewise. Our family are now adults as I write this, but together we have built wonderful memories that we are adding to year by year—including kayaking in flooded paddocks after too much rain, birthday parties, learning to drive, planting kiwifruit vines, developing pastures, extended family Christmases, rugby balls breaking spoutings, cricket balls flying through windows, family dinners with everyone squeezed around the table all talking at once, to name just a few. Life has been wonderful and messy and unpredictable, with moments of grandeur and moments of deep pain. But I hope my story ultimately leaves you with a sense of hope and the knowledge that when we each have the opportunity to be who we truly are—knowing that we are valued and worthy of love and acceptance—it is a beautiful gift to be treasured all the days of our lives.

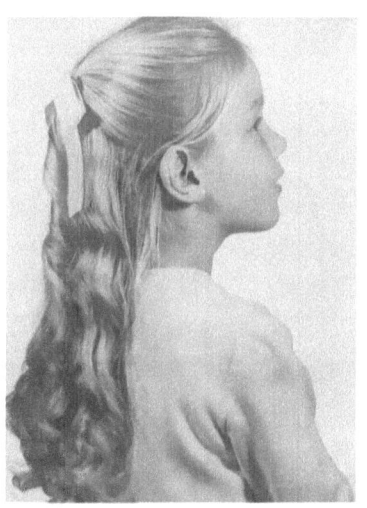

Me as a little girl, with my straight hair curled to be like 'Pollyanna' style. This is a photo I look at often and say a prayer for anyone who needs help to understand their adoption journey.

Acknowledgements

FIRSTLY, THANK YOU TO my foster parents. Thank you for giving me a home in the interim while everyone was figuring out what to do with this newborn baby girl. You are only briefly mentioned in my story, but thank you for taking care of me, as little Sheri, for the beginning weeks of my life.

Thank you to my writing buddies. You have supported me along the way, motivating me to push through the angst and keep writing, writing, writing. You encouraged me over the finish line. Thanks!

To dear friends who have believed in this story coming to light, even when there were hurdles and challenges. Thank you for nudging me when caution would hold me back. Some (you know who you are) would say "I wish we could be sisters", trusting the search for extended family was a good idea and a God-idea, helping me see the bigger picture. You each in your own way have added beauty to my life. Thanks for never doubting reunion was best for everyone, and for motivating me to share this story with others. Special thanks to Chris for being like a sister to me for many years. Your friendship is a treasure. And thank you, Donna and Jonny, for your unconditional love and friendship. The faith and strength you warmly share, highlight the God-colours in life.

To my brothers and sisters, both adopted and biological—you are valued and loved. Thank you for understanding that whether we've grown up together or 'found' each other later in life, the connection is important.

Thanks to all of you for considering the many different sides of adoption and for the conversations and validation. And thanks to my 'new' family for your warm welcome and acceptance. We might have had years apart, but it is lovely making up for lost time now, thank you.

For the gift of counsellors and coaches who have helped bring healing and steered me in a better direction when I needed it—thank you for listening, understanding and giving me oxygen when I most needed it. Big thanks to Ali—you helped me to look back, ensuring I could eventually move forward and helping me bring this book to life.

Thank you, Anya and Jeff McKee and the team at Torn Curtain Publishing. Anya, from day one, as I tentatively described my adoption story, you have walked with me one step at a time and found ways to make sense of my words; and Jeff, thank you for having patience with my many book design ideas and questions. Your expertise is warmly appreciated.

Thank you to my parents, natural and adoptive—two who gave me life, and two who lived with and supported me as I grew. Either way, thank you for giving me life. Ours is a complex story, deserving respect and compassion on all sides.

To my own dear family, some of our stories have been reserved away in my heart for now, stored for another time perhaps, or for conversations over family dinners, which usually result in beautiful chaos and hilarity. Thank you for cheering me on and believing in this book. You are all champions, and my heart is always for each one of you. My world is rich because you are in it, thank you all.

And to my Phil, you have been in this for the long haul, in every season, sunshine and storm. Thank you for your love and patience, strength and dependability. Thank you for believing in God with me and trusting He is 'for us and not against us'. Thank you for believing in this book and believing in the threads of love and light woven through it. You will always have my heart.

About the Author

LYNNE LIVES WITH HER husband on an orchard in the sunny Bay of Plenty, New Zealand. They enjoy sharing their life with their grown family who live nearby, which has happily expanded in recent years with several grandchildren. Lynne has a keen interest in family life and in 2021, Lynne was awarded a Diploma in Family Support from the Bethlehem Tertiary Institute.

Follow Lynne on social media at:
www.facebook.com/lynne.leppard.author

For speaking requests or to get in touch with the author, please email:
leppardlynne@gmail.com